WARFARE IN WOODS AND FORESTS

WARFARE
IN WOODS AND FORESTS

Anthony Clayton

FOREWORD BY
General Charles Guthrie,
The Lord Guthrie of Craigiebank
(formerly United Kingdom Chief of Defence Staff)

INDIANA UNIVERSITY PRESS

Bloomington & Indianapolis

This book is a publication of

Indiana University Press
601 North Morton Street
Bloomington, Indiana 47404-3797 USA

iupress.indiana.edu

Telephone orders   800-842-6796
Fax orders   812-855-7931
Orders by e-mail   iuporder@indiana.edu

∞ The paper used in this publication meets the minimum requirements of
the American National Standard for Information Sciences—Permanence
of Paper for Printed Library Materials, ANSI Z39.48–1992.

Manufactured in the United States of America

Library of Congress Cataloging-in-Publication Data

Clayton, Anthony.
Warfare in woods and forests / Anthony Clayton.
p. cm.
Includes bibliographical references and index.
ISBN 978-0-253-35688-8 (hbk. : alk. paper)—
ISBN 978-0-253-00553-3 (ebook) 1. Forest warfare—History.
2. Infantry drill and tactics—History. 3. Guerrilla warfare—History. I.
Title.
U167.5.F6C63   2011
355.4—dc23   2011020215
1 2 3 4 5   17 16 15 14 13 12

IN MEMORIAM

Judith

1940–2005

"We warred," wrote one at Spotsylvania,

"against a forest" and for all their guns the

forest won. The wounded burned in leaves.

The dead were hung like Indian dead in

baskets, root and bough. The trees buried

them, regrew as neither army did.

—MICHAEL MOTT, "DRIVING THROUGH THE WILDERNESS,
NORTH VIRGINIA IN A BLIZZARD TO RACHMANINOV"

CONTENTS

TERRAIN MAPS

FOREWORD

GENERAL CHARLES GUTHRIE,
THE LORD GUTHRIE OF CRAIGIEBANK
(FORMERLY UNITED KINGDOM CHIEF OF DEFENCE STAFF)

ANTHONY CLAYTON'S *Warfare in Woods and Forests* is a timely reminder of the difficulties facing those who may have to fight in the wooded areas that cover large tracts of the globe. Although some of the great military thinkers such as Clausewitz and Jomini have touched on such operations, and though some of the most decisive battles have been fought in woods and forests, surprisingly little literature and guidance are available compared to that which addresses the tactics and techniques to be employed in other types of warfare. This has much to do with the fact that formed conventional and uniformed armies did not wish to be delayed, ambushed, and constrained by an enemy that they found difficult to identify and place, and whose numbers they could not estimate. The policy, whenever possible, was to bypass, encircle, and maintain the momentum of the advance. The attitude was similar to that adopted toward street fighting and clearing buildings.

Today intelligence and information may be easier to collect because of technical development, and weapon systems may be more devastating, but difficulties remain when engaged in combat in forests. Irregular forces will take advantage afforded to them by wooded country, as the Chechens have demonstrated in the Caucasus. The chances of irregular forces eventually succeeding may not be great, but their opportunities are likely to be far greater than they would be in the open.

Anthony Clayton uses many historical examples to illustrate this book, starting with the annihilation of the Roman army of the Legate Quintilius Varus by Arminius at the Battle of the Teutoberger Wald in

AD 9 and ending with the ongoing wars in Chechnya. They all bring out the problems of this type of warfare.

If, as many say, the wars of the future are to be among the people, this book deserves serious study.

PREFACE

ON A WARM SUMMER DAY in 1943 my school contingent of the British Army's Officer Training Corps went out on an exercise, the only exercise of the corps that I can remember. We were led by our headmaster, splendid in his uniform of a captain in the Home Guard, a local defense militia raised to counter the threat of a German invasion. A classics scholar, he was a figure of awe to us fifteen and sixteen year olds. The exercise, set in the beautiful countryside in the West of England, was one of clearing a wood. The lucky among us were posted to lie in the sun at the edges of the wood representing machine gunners tasked to enfilade the notional enemy in flight out of the wood. The unlucky ones, which included myself, formed an extended line across the wood trampling through the trees, roots, brambles, and undergrowth with our "Drill Purpose Only" old rifles at the ready. I recall it clearly, as at the time it seemed so surgical and simple a military operation.

This memory has now led me, many years later, to write this book, studies of real fighting in and around woods and forests. In doing so I quickly came to appreciate that in practice such fighting was exceedingly difficult, and any commanders who thought it simple were likely to kill a great many of their own men. The chapters that follow look at a selection of soldiers' experiences of fighting among the trees in some of the combats over two thousand years, from the Teutoburger Wald Battle of AD 9 to the Chechnya conflict of AD 2009; it is limited to warfare in Europe and North America. Of special interest are issues such as how well prepared—or ill prepared—were soldiers and their officers, the tactics, the weapons, and the particularly brutal psychological dimension evident in some battles. The chapters therefore concentrate on the varying forms of forest battles, as space does not allow for more than a brief outline of the wider plans, campaigns, and wars in which the battles took place. Inevitably, during the centuries of personal armor, battles in forests and woods were fewer in number, as the early chapters show.

Works exist on jungle, desert, and urban warfare, but woods and forests have received little attention. Vivid material exists, however, in a variety of sources, among them theorists, memoirs, formation and regimental histories, and photographs. Surprising continuities appear, not least of which was the suicide of three senior commanders who had lost a battle in or around a forest: the Roman Legions' commander Varus in AD 9, the hapless Russian general Alexander Samsonov in 1914, and one of Adolf Hitler's favorite generals, Walter Model, in early 1945. Readers will recognize several others.

A number of campaigns and battles are described in this book. The selection of terrain maps from these operations has been made for their particular value in showing the strategic or tactical importance of the local forests and woods.

ACKNOWLEDGMENTS

THIS WORK COULD NEVER HAVE been written without the help of Andrew Orgill, John Pearce, and Ken Franklin at the Central Library of the British Royal Military Academy Sandhurst. My thanks to them all are profound, not only for the provision of abundant source material but for much encouragement.

I am also greatly indebted—for advice, ideas, and help—to General André Bach of the French Army, now retired, Matthew Bennet, Lieutenant-Colonel Charles Blandy, Paul Harris, Sean Kearney, Lieutenant-Colonel Ronnie McCourt, Martin Middlebrook, Professor Michael Mott, Sean Murray, W. North, Michael Orr, M. Phillipe Richardot, Lieutenant-General Jonathon Riley, Major P. Streit of the Swiss Army, Patrick Takle, and Professor H. P. Willmott. I am also very grateful to Ben Phillips of the University for Creative Arts, Farnham, for his careful preparation of the terrain maps.

The poem "Driving through the Wilderness, North Virginia in a Blizzard to Rachmaninov," from which the epigraph to the book is taken, is published in *Woman and the Sea: Selected Poems by Michael Mott* (Tallahassee: Anhinga, 1998). The author's dedication for my copy of this anthology book marks our fifty-year-long friendship.

Finally, an especial thanks to two people without whom this work would not have seen the light of day. John Card guided me through much of the unknown world of preparing an electronic manuscript; without his help, advice, and interest, the technology would have defeated me. And the patience and hard work of Gillian James, always undismayed by my endless text alterations and inelegant handwriting, was invaluable in bringing this work to fruition. The difficulties she faced, and my enormous gratitude for all the work she has done, should not be underestimated.

Thank you to my editor, Robert Sloan, and the editorial staff at Indiana University Press.

WARFARE IN WOODS AND FORESTS

Fig. 1.1 Soviet tanks in a wagon-train circle on the perimeter of a motti after a Finnish counter-offensive. See chapter 8. (Courtesy of the General Headquarters, Finnish Army)

Introduction

ARMY COMMANDERS AT ANY LEVEL from general to lieutenant do not like woods or forests. No one knows for certain who or what may be concealed among the trees: ambushes, regiments preparing for a sudden flank attack, stay-behind special forces or other units tasked to strike at an advancing army's rear guard, lines of logistic support, or just simply concealed observation posts watching and reporting their adversary's movements from the forest's edge. Until very recently, inside a forest all the advantages have lain with the defender even if his force is much smaller, provided he has made a careful plan and pre-positioned and concealed his men. An attacker is likely to find it exceedingly difficult to reconnoiter, and later to retain control of his men, particularly if the forest has thick undergrowth; his attack will lose vital momentum. Perhaps as few as one hundred yards into a wood, soldiers may lose sight of one another and their officers, sometimes also losing their own sense of direction. Traditional fire and movement tactics become impossible to control and coordinate. When brought under fire soldiers will run for cover, no longer keeping in line. Some, in fright, may well decide not to advance any farther or to retreat to safety. Terrifying noise may prevent shouted or even bugle orders from being heard. Among trees, radio signals equipment may deaden or not function at all. Flat trajectory weapons fired by either side will be deflected, malfunction, or send splinters flying dangerously. If forests are large, maintaining basic food and water supplies for an attacking army can soon become a serious problem, especially in extreme cold or heat. Unless there are roads, tracks, or beaten paths, the use of wheeled vehicles from chariots to tanks is nearly always impossible in woods; horses may be of more use. Tracks can also be easily blocked. Most frightening of all is the sudden unnerving appearance of enemy soldiers from behind trees or from undergrowth inflicting heavy casualties, perhaps encircling small groups of attackers.

Thus, if circumstances permit, a wise commander will try to avoid being led into a forest battle. Alternatively, again if ground conditions are suitable, he may try to use the locations of woods or forests to maneuver his opponent's forces into fighting on more open ground of his own choice. A defender will do the same, and either side may consider other possible uses of woods or forests on the edges of the main battleground. Nevertheless, as this book shall establish, operations within big woods or forests from the age of spears, pikes, and lances to the age of helicopters and heat-detection equipment have been necessary. They form a particular and costly form of warfare meriting as much special study as urban or desert fighting. Only comparable in any way is jungle warfare, but even here there are differences to be noted shortly.

Last but by no means least, forests can provide timber for a whole variety of military purposes: forts and strong points, bridges, pit props to strengthen trench systems, and material for creating obstacles to prevent the movement of men, wagons, vehicles, and later tanks. Peculiar to forest warfare was the abatti, a barrier of tree trunks, pointed at their ends, facing an enemy.

The chapters that follow consider wood and forest battles both large and small in different periods over the last two thousand years in Europe and North America. Generally the smaller the wood, the easier the battle, and the larger the forest, the more difficult. In each age the fighting has taken three main forms: battles of formations or units within woods and forests, the much more common use of woods for the mounting of flank attacks or for refuge in adversity, and irregular or forest-based guerrilla operations. Where experience of forest fighting has led to theoretical writings or doctrines within the period covered by the chapter, these are summarized. For example, some academics, usually Marxist, have argued that guerrilla warfare demonstrates the essential union of front and rear. Forest warfare, however, has generally been treated by both theorists and peacetime staff officers and military planners as the ugly stepchild, with soldiers only rarely trained properly for it.[1]

Further, until the mid-eighteenth century, with the exception of the citizen soldiers of Switzerland, armies were ill-equipped for forest warfare. Few commanders had any relevant experience. In addition, there was an absence of what is now called "topographical intelligence"; either nobody knew or thought to bother about collecting such information. Maps that showed useful details of roadways and villages would vaguely show forest areas colored green but with little or no detail. As late as the First and Second World Wars, prewar picture postcards were sometimes the only material available.

A wide variety of topographical factors, however, have greatly influenced all forest fighting. Among these factors has been the strategic or tactical importance of a particular forest or wood; its size, its shape, the age of its trees and their general condition, and undergrowth such as bracken; whether the area was on flat or hilly land or on solid, swampy, or rocky ground; whether the edges of the wooded area were neatly defined with open ground in front or whether there were spurs of trees or saplings running out into brushwood; the weather, the seasons, and the colors of the year (particularly affecting deciduous forests); the heights and thickness of the trees, big trees offering concealment for two or three defenders preparing an ambush; the forest's density effect on humidity and light or a forest gloom, and, in war, the ability to fire artillery shells effectively within the forest; any significant animal life; and, finally, the existence of possible passages through the forest, single- or double-track roads, paths, glades, rides, or clearings that could facilitate the movement of light artillery, cavalry, and later armor or infantry.[2] In some cases, one or more local conditions could make a forest virtually impassable, even for a foot soldier; in others, known tracks and paths could suddenly become impassable following a heavy rainstorm—or a broken-down vehicle. Tanks and bulldozers can clear smaller trees, but a resulting foliage pileup may impede or block further progress. Maintaining supplies, food, fodder for horses or fuel for vehicles, and ammunition, as well as evacuating casualties and guarding any prisoners taken, quickly become acute problems. Few commanders will opt to add to these difficulties with the risk of a forest battle at night. All these factors had to be borne in mind by commanders leading an attack. A commander might have to commit many more men to clear a forest area than the defender had deployed—a calculation to be set against the overall correlation of forces in the area.

Many of these elements appear, of course, in jungle warfare, generally in magnified forms such as the conditions of a tropical climate, medical problems, the day-to-day health of the expatriate soldiers, and even greater logistic and supply problems. But overall the biggest difference remains the huge size of historic battle areas which may be almost nationwide, such as Burma, Malaya, and Indonesia, far larger than the biggest forest areas of Europe or even North America. These, paradoxically, provide an advantage to the attacker, as the defender is unsure of his opponent's plans and priorities—this in contrast to the defender's advantage in smaller-scale woods or forests.[3] The difference, of course, is much less in jungle areas such as Vietnam, where conditions were at times comparable to those in Europe.

In certain campaigns armies that arrived on the scene of a forest operation created new units in the light of their experience, using knowledgeable foreign officers when necessary and available. These units then had to be equipped with special uniforms and weapons. At the end of the campaign, however, such units often found themselves absorbed into their nation's line infantry with little or no recognition of their earlier skills; the British King's Royal Rifle Corps, founded as the Royal American Regiment, and the Light Infantry battalions and regiments are examples. Weapons, communication, and supply facilities for forest warfare were also rarely maintained during peacetime, requiring a nation to improvise when it later became necessary. One notable exception to this was Finland's army in 1939. In contrast to this absence of prewar preparation and wartime improvisation and development is the growth of effective forest-based partisan warfare, the most striking example being the Soviet Union in its 1941–45 war. Yet modern, high-tech land warfare developments post-1945 have almost certainly reduced many of the traditional advantages held by defenders against attackers unless the defenders' own forces have been equipped with equally modern counter-technology protection. The opposing technologies are summarized in chapter 9.

Finally, as readers shall soon come to see, the theoretical writing on forest warfare over time has sometimes developed into doctrine. The first genuinely clear analysis and instructions appeared in the eighteenth century, with others following in the nineteenth century. Yet, with regard to Europe and North America, little theoretical writing emerged in the twentieth century, primarily because the rapid advance of air and armor technology bypassed the need for theory, just as tanks and aircraft can sweep by or over wooded areas. Perhaps only the guerrilla and his opponent are now likely to wage war from woodland or forest.

Warfare before Firearms

THE FIRST DECADE OF THE FIRST millennium AD saw a violent forest battle that was to have great significance for Western Europe. In this battle, in a forest near Osnabrück in western Germany, an army of the Roman Empire planning to make the river Elbe, further east, an imperial boundary suffered a catastrophic defeat.[1]

At this time, AD 9, the Roman garrison in western Germany consisted of five legions, each just under four thousand well-trained men supported by some ten thousand local auxiliaries, supply personnel, laborers, and camp followers of every kind. Each legion was composed of infantry cohorts of eighty men, and some also had a small number of horsemen. Each legion infantry man was armed with a short sword for stabbing, a dagger, and a javelin-throwing spear. For protection, he carried a large curved shield made of layers of wood covered in felt, with armor covering his body from the neck to just above the knees, and a helmet. This equipment, cumbersome and heavy, was designed for close-quarter fighting in open country; it was to prove a serious disadvantage in a forest.

In the summer of AD 9 three of the five legions under the command of Publius Quintilius Varus, an officer both inefficient and ineffective, had been asserting a Roman presence in the Minden area. Under cover of service with the auxiliaries was a German Cheruscan nobleman, Arminius, who, for both nationalist and personal reasons, was planning an uprising against the Romans. The three legions, the XVII, XVIII, and XIX, were planning to retire to winter quarters on the Lippe River when a small local uprising broke out near the Weser River. Arminius persuaded Varus to deal with the uprising by passing through the Teu-toburger Wald, a rough terrain of ridges and defiles where the hills were covered with thick forest, mainly oak. Varus was warned against Arminius and advised to avoid the area, but he refused to alter his plans. Consequently he fell into a trap set by Arminius who knew the area well. Arminius led the march at the outset but soon defected, accompanied by many of the auxiliaries, to join the insurgents.

Varus had no concept of topographical intelligence, in this case a matter of leading the legions through dense forest along a steep nar-row track in conditions made even worse by heavy rain, strong wind, and fallen trees. Arminius, who had rallied a very large number to his cause, perhaps as many as fifty thousand German tribesmen, fell first upon detachments sent out by Varus to deal with the uprising; these were massacred. He next attacked the main column, its movements carefully watched by men in the forest. The attack was launched from all sides—on the advance guard trying to prepare a road for the wagons, on the flank guards, and, finally, on the rear guard and those of the follow-ers who had not defected or fled into the forest. The Romans, in reply, followed their standard operational procedure and hurriedly build an earthwork fort only to become surrounded.

Arminius, however, was well acquainted with Roman methods and, rather than mount a siege, he let them attempt, on the next day, to march out. Varus, who had been wounded, tried to lead the march but was met by a barrier of fallen trees, forcing the Romans back to their earthwork fort after suffering heavy casualties. The more mobile, fast-moving Ger-mans simply threw crude darts and spears at the heavily encumbered legion infantrymen as they stumbled around. Heavy rainfall increased the weight of the felt on the Romans' shields. Arminius apparently also knew where to strike to cause the greatest confusion, namely, the boundary lines between the three legions and the horsemen. Wounded by spears and darts, the horses plunged back into the infantry throw-ing their riders. The Germans quickly took control at the fort, storming the trench and log defenses and cutting down the Roman soldiers with their broadswords. Varus ordered the legions to retreat, but, in the for-est, the cohorts soon split up, the commanders having lost control in the broken ground and dense forest. Fighting became that of isolated groups

struggling for their lives, as mass numbers of Germans emerged from
the hills to attack with the utmost ferocity against which the terrified
legion soldiers were powerless. Heavy shields and body armor could
not protect the whole body against the hailstorm of German darts and
spears. Varus himself committed suicide. An attempt by the remaining horsemen to escape was also halted, the horses losing their footing
among the trees and stumps. The few survivors were enslaved or tor-
tured, or both, and the officers were sacrificed to the gods. Rome lost at
least seventeen thousand legion soldiers and auxiliaries in a battle they
probably would have won had it been fought in open ground. The battle
itself set the pattern—one of dread, determination, and death—for
many forest battles to follow.

The certain result of this battle was that the Romans could no longer
assert any lasting control of Germany across the Rhine, and they soon
abandoned any efforts to do so. In Rome the aged Emperor Augustus
was frequently heard to lament, "Vare, Vare, Redde legiones" ("Varus,
Varus, give me back my legions"). The victory, later perceived by German nationalists as one of proto-nationalism, is celebrated in German
history, with thousands of German boys over the centuries being named
Hermann. The argument has also been advanced that the failure of
the Romans to make Germany a Roman province set a precedent for
the future. Germany was now destined to be different from the other
post-1648 Westphalian nations, and it was thought that the Romans
would have prevented the Anglo-Saxon migration to Britain. Nevertheless, Teutoburger Wald was sufficiently decisive without historical
might-have-beens.

MONS GRAUPIUS

Rome learned two lessons from the Teutoburger wars. One was
strategic: to base the expansion of the empire's frontiers on a profit or
loss basis and not to overstretch. The other was the importance of select-
ing able generals. Tacitus describes the very competent Gnaius Julius
Agricola before and during the battle of Mons Graupius in Scotland (the
precise location is disputed) in AD 83. Addressing his soldiers before
the battle, Agricola admitted that he lacked "exact local knowledge"
but urged his two legions onward: "We have our hands and our swords

in them and, with this, we have all that matters." After repelling Briton attacks on his legions and using his auxiliary infantry and cavalry, Agricola turned his attention on the Britons who had fled into the woods:

> Agricola was everywhere at once. He ordered the cohorts to rally, discard their equipment, and ring the woods like hunters. Where the woods were dense, dismounted cavalry went in to scour them; where they were thinner, the cavalry did the work. But the Britons, when they saw our ranks steady and firm and the pursuit beginning again, simply turned and ran. They no longer kept any formation or any touch with one another but deliberately broke into small groups to reach their far and trackless retreats. Only night and exhaustion ended the pursuit. Of the enemy some 10,000 fell, on our side 360.[2]

Tacitus's account points to features that will reappear frequently in later chapters: Agricola's regret at his lack of topographical intelligence, the need for soldiers to discard equipment that could get caught up in the branches of trees, and the importance of cohesion.

MEDIEVAL WARFARE

In the long centuries of sword, shield, arrow, spear, pike, and lance, before foot soldiers were equipped with muskets, there was only a limited number of each of the three main categories of warfare in or around forests. Knights in armor and foot soldiers with a pike or bow were of limited efficiency among trees, and commanders lacked the means of control to retain command. Forests were not generally the scene of a battle among the trees but, on occasion, could be useful for an ambush or a flank attack, and for guerrilla warfare. Frequently—for example, at Bannockburn and Crécy—woods or forests formed the "defining edge" of a battlefield.

An early surprise attack launched the Battle of Roncesvalles Pass in 778, which devastated the rear guard of the army of Charlemagne led by Roland, at the time returning from Spain to France after fighting the Saracens. The Frankish rear guard had fallen behind, probably because of plunder amid the baggage train, and was ambushed by Basques streaming out from wooded slopes on either side of the pass road. Although Charlemagne's men were superior both in number and weaponry, the surprise assault and their disadvantaged position in the

Nive Valley Pass led to their all being massacred before help could reach them. By then the Basques had retired into the forest.

An early example of forest-based raiding is that of the Magyars, who swept westward across central Europe in the tenth century. The Magyars were lightly equipped mounted archers simply out for plunder who did not want a formal engagement and withdrew into the woods to avoid one. Their raiding activities became serious in 899 in Venetia and in 900 in Bavaria, later moving further into Provence, Alsace, and northern France. Their tactics were based on agility and mobility. Bands of a hundred or more would stream out of a wood, occasionally deploying a small force apparently willing to fight a punitive group of pursuers only to retreat and lure them into an ambush, where they would suddenly be confronted by superior numbers pouring out of the woods on both front and rear flanks. For some fifty years, resistance against the Magyar raids was carried out by equally fast-riding cavalry groups who would pursue the raiders into the woods, also making use of fortified encampments or castles to control an area. The Magyar scourge only ended in 955 at the hands of the Holy Roman Emperor Otto the Great after two battles in southern Germany.

Resistance to Anglo-Norman operations and campaigns to conquer Wales, Scotland, and Ireland was based on the same general principles of agility and mobility, often by irregular guerrillas and with forays mounted from woods, which knights in armor on horseback found difficult or impossible to contain, even if greatly superior in number.

Welsh attacks on the Normans began as early as the last decades of the eleventh century and were to continue for more than two hundred years. Southern Welsh irregular bands fought using bows and arrows, whereas men from the North preferred long spears; both could penetrate armor or wound a horse. To preserve agility, they wore light armor or protective clothing and carried only a small shield. Blaring trumpets would inspire the insurgents' assaults, but the bands preferred to melt away into the woods rather than face a pitched encounter. In his two big campaigns, Edward I had to employ several hundred carpenters and laborers to clear the way through the woods for a road to Flint and also to cut down sanctuary forests. The final stabilization rested on the construction of strongholds, later castles, which could dominate, if not totally control, the forests and countryside.

The Scots seized the opportunity of a temporary loosening of the Norman kings control in northern England caused by the Conquest and the twelfth-century civil war to launch raids for slaves and plunder. The raiders, more irregulars than the later army, were equipped with spears, javelins, and knives. Like the Welsh, they avoided a pitched encounter until 1138. The English then adopted the same strategy as in Wales, making use of fortified strongholds, or *mottes*, which were wooden towers set on a hillock encircled by a ditch and palisade, from which horsemen could sally forth in pursuit of raiders.[3] Woods retained their importance when Scotland raised a more effective national army. Robert Bruce's early campaigns from 1307 to 1309 were guerrilla based, one tactic being the use of groups sallying forth from forests to attack supply lines to English garrisons. In more open warfare—and after the death of Edward I—the Battle of Bannockburn in 1314 brought out the significance of the intelligent use of the terrain. Bruce forced the significantly larger twenty-three-thousand-strong English Army to fight on too small a front, just slightly over a mile, between an enormous marsh morass called the Carse on the east and, on the west, the forested areas of New Park and Gillies Hill. The battle, as is well known, was decided by the inability of the English cavalry, unwisely placed in the lead, to pass through the lines of Scottish pikemen and the equal inability of the English archers placed behind the cavalry to strike off at the Scots pikemen with any effect: confusion and chaos ensued. An attempt by some English archers to enter the forest and attack the Scots' right flank was foiled. Finally, an unplanned spontaneous descent from their cover among the trees of Gillies Hill by followers of the Scots camp who had seized any weapon available completed the English rout.

Events in Ireland were rather different. The country's terrain was even more difficult than that of Wales in terms of woods and marshes, and the numbers, formal or informal, of Anglo-Norman invaders was considerably smaller. The Irish had a tradition of local regional conflict and cattle raiding among themselves, which, with full local knowledge, was easily adapted into raids and ambushes against invaders and settlers. In the case of an invasion in the woods, the Irish devised "plashing," the stringing and intertwining of tree branches to link woods together, or along and across roads. Plashing forced any invader to halt and become a target for attack from the front and from the flanks. Sir Charles Oman, in his *History of the Art of War,* notes that this tactic caused the Anglo-Norman armored knights great difficulties; the weakness of the Irish, however, was their lack of protective armor, their reluctance to stand firm in open ground, and their inadequate weaponry, limited to a few darts, a short spear (but no pikes), hand axes, and poor archery skills. They were also vulnerable to ruses such as feigned retreats, surprise assaults, and flank attacks by horsemen. The result was that the Anglo-Norman conquerors built castles and claimed land; the Irish withdrew to the woods and marshlands—a social and economic structure that not only precluded development but also laid the foundations of centuries of strife.[4]

Forest-based resistance and the tactics to deal with it were similar elsewhere in Europe. Charlemagne used mixed units of knights in armor and foot soldiers with swords and spears in anti-guerrilla pursuit groups. Further east, ambushes from forests harassed the German Order of Teutonic Knights in their mid-thirteenth-century advance into Poland and Lithuania. A notable leader in the Hundred Years' War was Bertrand du Guesclin, who initially led small but later much larger bands from woods to attack the English in Brittany. On one occasion he disguised a small band as simple woodcutters and captured a castle. His bands moved swiftly across the country attacking English garrison lines of communication and food convoys. In the final stage of his Brittany campaign in the 1370s du Guesclin used mercenaries, known as *routiers,* in his bands in order to make Brittany ungovernable and force an English withdrawal.

The fourteenth-century also saw three battles—Crécy in 1346, Poitiers in 1356, and the less well-known Aljubarrata in 1385—in which the eventual victories, most obviously spurred by the longbow's superior range technology, was also the result of the victors' use of woods and forests when making their plans for battle. At Crécy Edward III led an English and Welsh army of ten thousand against a numerically superior but poorly organized army of some twenty thousand led by Philip VI. By marching his army along a narrow path through the Forest of Crécy, a path that Philip could not dare risk pursuing, Edward was able to take up a defensive position near the Village of Crécy. His southwestern right and rear flanks shielded by woods and his northeastern flank by steep terraced hillsides, Edward's defensive position denied Philip the chance to deploy his larger force. Philip's failed attack led to chaos, and the English longbow arrows turned chaos into catastrophe.

Poitiers, where the Black Prince's army of six thousand was attempting to withdraw toward Bordeaux while faced by King John II's army of at least eighteen thousand, was, above all, a battle fought in thickets and scrub. The Black Prince's use of the terrain enabled him to conceal the deployment of his men-at-arms and archers at the outset, while the Nouaille Wood secured his rear from attack. The thickets and dead ground also concealed the audacious Gascon Cavalry flank march around a hill for a final decisive attack on the French left and rear.

The issue at stake at Aljubarrata was the independence of Portugal under its monarch Joao I, whom King John of Castile wished to subdue.[5] John's army was considerably larger than Joao's, but the latter made his tactical decisions with the aid of his English advisers. He chose a reentry position between the two spurs and then planted archers and crossbowmen masked by trees and protected by trees that had been cut down to secure his flanks. The Castilians, in badly coordinated attacks, attempted to rush the center and were mowed down by arrows, javelins, and crossbow bolts from the flanks.

The fifteenth century saw developments foreshadowing the future of war technology evident in the century's two major battles involving forests. At Agincourt, in 1415, artillery first appeared in the form of bombards capable of projecting iron or stone balls, some more than five hundred pounds in weight, against castle walls. By 1476, at the battle of Morat, a Burgundian army was well provided with light guns mounted on wheeled carriages.

AGINCOURT

The Battle of Agincourt, fought on 25 October 1415 between the English Army of Henry V and the French Army commanded by Charles d'Albret, Constable of France, was one in which terrain proved more important than numbers.[6] The French Army totaled some 25,000 men, of whom 3,000 were crossbowmen, together with 7,000 mounted and 15,000 dismounted men-at-arms and knights. The English totaled fewer than 5,500 men, 4,500 longbow archers, and 750 knights and men-at-arms.

The men-at-arms in both armies were knights and squires. Essentially horsemen, they mostly carried a long sword; some also carried a six-foot poleax with an ax head or a shortened lance. All wore armor from helmet to ankles. The crossbowmen's rate of fire was two- to three-foot-long bolts per minute, and a good longbowman could manage up to a dozen arrows.

Henry was well informed about his enemy; the French were over-confident and light-hearted. The English were unfit and weary after seventeen days of marching but were inspired, if not in Shakespearean terms, by their king. Most important, however, was Henry's decision to fight on a front of some one thousand yards in an open if somewhat marshy plain flanked on the west by the Forest of Agincourt and on the east by the Forest of Trainecourt. This decision made classic use of forests to force a much superior adversary to fight on ground where that superiority could not be used to advantage. Henry took further advantage by advancing close to the French lines and at the same time dispatching some longbowmen into the flanking woods and including others in wedge-shaped detachments protected by sharpened wooden stakes in his own front line. An opening French cavalry charge against the English flanks met with the first of several hailstorms of arrows from the longbowmen. Each man carried at least twenty-five arrows and perhaps as many as fifty; their discharge in well controlled volleys could loose as many as five thousand arrows at ten-second intervals. Long-bowmen shooting from the woods would have shot with an overhead curved trajectory. Although the French horsemen's armor generally protected them, the arrows felled the horses, leading to confusion. Disorder was compounded following later French attacks by men-at-arms and cavalry meeting the same hail of arrows. The French cavalry was further held up by the wooden stakes, thus becoming a special target for the longbowmen. As a result, the massive French force was pushed into a chaotic melee of dismounted men, foot soldiers, and crossbow-men. The English bowmen in the woods discarded their bows to join in the hand-to-hand fighting with their swords, massacring the totally disorganized French Army.

While the whirring and whistling sounds of the arrow volleys, the clang of arrows striking metal, the yells of the wounded, and the bay-ing of the fallen horses all contributed to the destruction of the French,

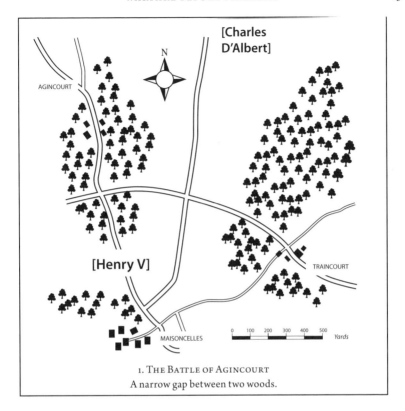

1. THE BATTLE OF AGINCOURT
A narrow gap between two woods.

there must also have been an additional sense of panic arising from their being caught in a trap between the woods.

The massive English victory was to be marred by Henry's belief, after a French marauding attack on his rear camp at Maisoncelles, that a major French attack was to follow. Accordingly, he ordered that the many French prisoners held in the camp, a number still in their armor, to be killed, only rescinding the order when it was clear that no attack was coming.

MORAT

The French bombards had played no significant role at Agincourt, and even though well represented in the front line of the next great fifteenth-century battle, Morat, artillery was not able to be decisive. The Battle of Morat (or Murten) was fought on 22 June 1476 between Charles the Bold, Duke of Burgundy, and the soldiers of the eight Swiss

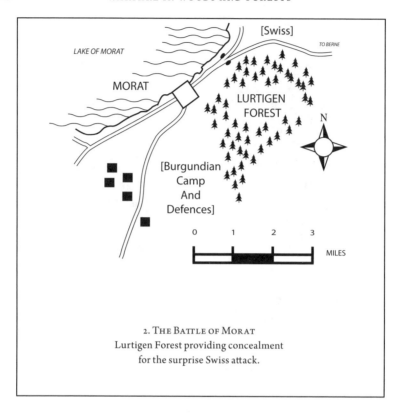

2. The Battle of Morat
Lurtigen Forest providing concealment
for the surprise Swiss attack.

Confederation statelets, each led by its cantonal commander and supported by the Duke of Lorraine.[7] The battle was to play a decisive role in the future of two countries, France and Switzerland. Burgundy was, in theory, a fiefdom of the Kingdom of France, but Charles was campaigning to expand the fiefdom's size with a view to an eventual independent kingdom. The two forces in the field were about equally matched in numbers, some twenty-four thousand each, although the Confederation had an additional two thousand under siege by the Burgundians in the town of Morat on the eastern shore of Morat Lake.

The majority of the Swiss foot soldiers were equipped with weaponry that proved successful in battles—pikes and pole-arms fifteen to eighteen feet long, some fitted with additional blades just below the sharp point of the pike or pole. A few from the wealthier cantons possessed an arquebus, the earliest form of a musket, but this had limited range and could not penetrate armor. Clothing varied, again with some of the wealthier soldiers wearing armor, but the majority did not even have a steel helmet. The Swiss were also very weak in cavalry, with only a small number of Austrian and Lorraine horsemen, and were even weaker in artillery. The Swiss style of fighting appears to have been very brutal both in battle and in the treatment of captives. Their most successful combat tactic was a swift advance in closely formed echelon squares, falling upon an opponent caught unaware and unprepared, and thus creating shock, terror, and panic.

The Burgundian force included numbers of cavalry detachments, light artillery, and a body of English longbow archers. Their three hundred light-artillery pieces had a limited rate of fire, at best seventy solid shot rounds per day. Further, before the battle, Charles had ordered the English longbow to be replaced by arbalests, a steel bolt-firing crossbow that could penetrate armor but had a much slower rate of fire. This late change of weaponry proved to be very unwise.

Although Charles had already suffered a setback at the Battle of Grandson earlier in the year, he remained fatally overconfident. For him, the Swiss were but "a nation of cowherds." His own army, however, was far from united, with much friction and hostility between different ethnic contingents. His battle plan was also seriously flawed. His best troops together with most of the artillery were concentrated on the immediate lakeside ground and on a hill overlooking the northern part of Morat. The remainder of his army was divided into two groups, one encircling the eastern center and the other the southeastern flank side of the town. The regiments in the center faced the big and dense Lurtigen Forest; those on the southeastern flank were protected by a hurriedly dug ditch and a hedge palisade. Charles expected that the battle would take the form of a strong Swiss lakeside attack, together with Swiss contingents arriving from Berne in an attempt to relieve the besieged and suffering town. He planned to repel such Swiss moves using his best and most trusted units and artillery, after which he would move on to occupy the town. A captured Swiss prisoner confirmed this expectation of the Swiss plans. Charles was therefore not greatly concerned that his army's various ethnic groups did not support one another.

Prior to the battle, the Burgundian artillery had bombarded the town as a prologue to an attack that the garrison was able to repel. The center and southeastern flanks had become slack, however. Patrols

Fig. 2.1. The Battle of Morat. Swiss contingents marching out of the Lurtigen Forest at prayer before their assault. (Details from a drawing by Evert van Muyven published in Colonel Emile Frey, *La Suisse sous les drapeaux*, Neuchatel ca. 1900)

reported only what they assumed to be the advance elements of a relieving force in the Lurtigen Forest. Patrolling a forest area is considerably more difficult than patrolling open ground, but Charles questioned neither the motivation nor the assiduity of the patrols. The next day, the 22nd, there was a heavy rain. Charles continued to presume that the Swiss were not ready for an attack, that rain would affect any powder-firing weapons they might have, and that any assault they might be planning would have to be postponed. He ordered a stand-down.

But what Charles had assumed to be an advance guard or a feint in the forest was, in fact, the rear guard of the main Swiss contingents assembling under cover of the trees. As the Burgundians were settling down for a comfortable midday meal, the first of the three massive columns—the vanguard, the main body, and the rear guard—of Swiss foot soldiers began pouring out of the Lurtigen Forest. The Burgundians had a mere ten to fifteen minutes to arm themselves and form up before the Swiss pikemen were on them. The Swiss columns successively swept through the Burgundians' right flank ditch and palisade, and the gap between the two Burgundian groups. Although the forty guns of the Burgundian artillery distributed in the area inflicted severe casualties on the advancing Swiss, the wrongly equipped Burgundians, taken by surprise, were overwhelmed by the pikes and polemen. Panic and a five-hour massacre followed, with Charles himself forced to take flight. Only a few detachments on the Burgundian left flank were able to escape up the road toward Berne. At least ten thousand and perhaps as many as twelve thousand Burgundian soldiers were killed or drowned in the lake while trying to escape.

In a letter to the Duke of Milan written after the battle, the Milanese ambassador to Burgundy, Panigarola, offers a firsthand observer's description of the Swiss tactics.[8] During the evening, before Panigarola had made his own reconnaissance, he encountered some Swiss skirmishers in the forest who had fired a few shots at his party. He had not been able to see any of the Swiss main bodies, but he later estimated that they had been concealed beneath folds in the forest ground. At the time, Charles had assessed the Swiss numbers as too few to pose a danger, despite Panigarola's advice that this might be a ruse and urging caution. Charles decided to defer any further battle plan decisions and, as there appeared to be no night activity, he took no further action the following morning. But during the night the Swiss contingent, silently and out of sight, had gradually made their way toward the edge of the forest. Panigarola's letter further describes the Swiss pouring out of the forest in serried ranks, all the foot soldiers armed with pikes or pole-arms, together with Alpine horn musicians and men carrying banners in the van. Between the lead units and the next contingents were some four hundred horsemen with very few light guns in support. The Swiss were greeted with artillery and crossbow fire, but they closed ranks and steadily gained ground. Panigarola and others estimated that at least eight thousand and possibly ten or more thousand men were in the three Swiss echelons that streamed out of the forest.

Morat dealt the mortal blow to the Burgundian cause. The following year, 1477, Charles died of wounds received during the siege of Nancy. Burgundy returned to being a French fief, and the Swiss cantons took another major step toward independence. In military history Morat remains one of the best examples of the use of a forest to achieve total surprise and a decisive victory.

THE FORD OF THE BISCUITS

Perhaps the last of the classic medieval-patterned battles involving forests was a small-scale engagement known as the Battle of the Ford of the Biscuits, fought in Ireland five miles south of Eniskillen on 7 August 1594 during the revolt of Hugh O'Donnell. The castle at Eniskillen was under siege by O'Donnell's forces, which included a small number of Scotsmen, probably mercenaries. An English force of six hundred infantry and forty-six cavalry troops under the command of Sir Henry Duke set forth to relieve the siege. They successfully crossed the Ford of Drumane on the river Arney without opposition. The horsemen leading the column moved round a densely wooded hill, the infantry and supply column following. The Irish, some one thousand strong led by Hugh Maguire, then sprung an ambush, bowmen fast firing into the English column from the wood and, finally, with loud yells, charging down the hill killing fifty-one and wounding sixty-nine English soldiers and looting the column's supply wagons and packhorse loads. From the number of biscuits taken by the victors the battle owes its name.[9]

Early Modern Warfare
1500–1713

—◁○/○/○▷—

EARLY MODERN WARFARE IN EUROPE was marked by the development of artillery and, for the foot soldier, the evolution from the fifteenth-century arquebus to the early-eighteenth-century muskets that had a longer range and the capability of penetrating armor. On the fields of battle over the sixteenth and seventeenth centuries, expensive men-at-arms in armor became progressively replaced by a more affordable foot-soldier infantry armed with very early muskets. In addition to the lesser cost, commanders were also thinking in terms of sieges, columns, and lines.

Neither the new weaponry nor the tactical formations resulting from these changes were in any way suited to forest warfare. Artillery remained flat trajectory, solid shot projectiles likely to hit as many trees as opponents. Forming lines and columns in infantry movements, essential to withstand a cavalry charge, was difficult or totally impossible in forests. Above all, the musket itself was an unwieldy weapon in thick forest and undergrowth. Although the design of the musket was to progress from the sixteenth-century matchlock, in which a slow-burning match was pushed into the powder pan, to the wheel locks and flintlocks of the seventeenth and eighteenth centuries, the musket's muzzle-loading barrels, three feet or more in length with a bayonet an additional foot long, were never easy to handle among trees. And making matters worse was the added length of the ramrod needed for reloading. A total of eight feet of space was therefore needed to load the musket, whether the musketeer was standing, kneeling, or, in an emergency, lying on the ground. That amount of clear space was only rarely at hand among trees and undergrowth. Moreover, it was absolutely vital that the powder be kept dry, a challenging task with forest conditions very often damp, trees dripping long after a rainfall had stopped. Men who were frightened or cold, even if well trained, might fumble among the trees, especially in a forest gloom. In addition, all muskets were noisy and smoky, and, if old or badly maintained, could be dangerous to the musketeer. The bayonet was at its most useful only in the hands of steady well-trained men. A defending soldier emerging from the cover of a tree and firing a round at an attacker and then following this up with his bayonet could be ter-rifying, psychologically, for the victim as well as his companions. These constraints meant that until the mid-eighteenth century few engage-ments were fought in forests, although several, including two major battles, used forests as concealment for attacks.

WITTSTOCK

The first of these two major battles—the Battle of Wittstock fought just south of the small northern German town of Pomerania on 4 Octo-ber 1636—was one of the most important in the Thirty Years' War.[1] The battle was between a Protestant Swedish Army of fifteen thousand, comprised of nine infantry brigades and fifty calvary squadrons, and their Catholic opponents, an Allied Army of some twenty thousand that included thirteen infantry brigades, seventy cavalry squadrons, and thirty-three guns. The Swedish Army was commanded by the very able General Johan Baner. The Allied Army, an alliance between Sax-ony and the Holy Roman Empire, had no commander. The battle was deployed on a ridge facing south and southeast with a six-ditch earthen defense system and a wall of linked wagons in the center; on the left was a wooded hill and further east the river Dosse. On the Allied right lay a heath and the large, dense oak forest of Heiligengrab. The imperial contingent under Marazinno held the Allied right; Saxony's Elector, John George, commanded the center with the artillery; and a brave but not very competent Saxon general, Melchior von Hatzfeldt, was in com-mand on the left. The quality of the Saxon contingents was mediocre.

The overall Swedish position in northern Germany was in serious danger. The Elector of Saxony had joined the imperial cause, and the Swedes retained only a small bridgehead in the north. The Swedish

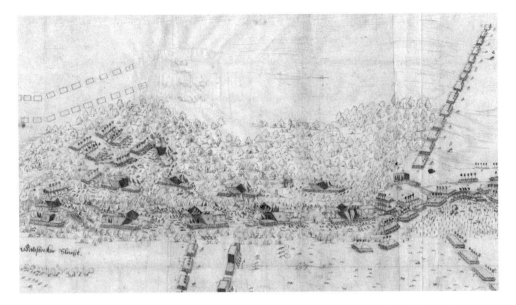

Fig. 3.1. The Battle of Wittstock. The Swedish army prepares for its assault on the wood defenses of the Allied center and left flank before Wittstock. (Detail from a 5-foot, 11-inch, illustration of the battle. Courtesy of the Swedish Krigsarkivet, Stockholm)

force, screened by thick woodlands, advanced on Wittstock from the south and crossed the Dosse River. General Baner, despite his numerical inferiority, launched an attack on the center and both flanks, using the tree-covered hills to best advantage. Recognizing his opponent's strength in the center, Baner's ploy was to approach the enemy concealed by the sandy, tree-covered hills, to mount an attack on the hill on the Allies' left flank, and then to move in on the centre, thereby weakening the Allies right flank and the right-side detachments of the center. At the same time a quarter of his force was to be deployed in a seven-mile ride encircling the Heiligengrab Forest to mount a surprise pincer attack on the Allied center and rear. The fighting on the Allies' left of center proved very severe, and the cavalry force, led by a Scots officer named James King, was delayed on its ride first by the marshy terrain and then by the trees and roots in the forest, arriving to save the day only in the nick of time. The Swedish cavalry, pouring out from around the edges of the forest, managed to completely surprise its opponent, first easily disposing of the screen of one thousand German musketeers and then descending on John George's and Hatzfeldt's center and rear, capturing their artillery. Dusk and darkness prevented the Swedes from fully following up on their success, but their achievement was nevertheless considerable. The Allied force withdrew in some disorder, losing more men in Baner's pursuit the following day.

Sweden's important position in northern Germany and its military reputation were restored; the victory, both spectacular and historic, was described with little exaggeration as a classic case of good command and control. The Battle of Wittstock thus made Sweden one of the winners in a war in which many of the other countries involved were massive losers.

MALPLAQUET

The War of the Spanish Succession, fought in the first decade of the eighteenth century, was the last of the early modern wars and would establish the reputation of John Churchill, Duke of Marlborough. It was Marlborough's last major battle, the Battle of Malplaquet, fought on 11 September 1709, in which forests would again play a significant role.[2]

Malplaquet was a village on the French side of the French-Belgian border, some nine miles south of Mons. The French Army, under the command of Marshals Claude Villars and Louis Boufflers, was ordered by King Louis XIV to secure the fortress of Mons, and thus prevent the Grand Alliance Army of the Duke of Marlborough and Prince Eugène from advancing on Paris. The French Army totaled 80,000 and that of the Alliance 110,000, including a significant superiority in infantry battalions, cavalry, and guns. To make his stand Villars chose a site just north of the village. There he could use two wooded areas to secure his flanks, on his left the Forest of Taisinière, or Sars, and on his right the smaller Lanières Forest; at the same time he could prepare a strong defense in the one-and-a half-mile gap in the center, with his cavalry in the rear. Marlborough's plan was to mount successive attacks on Villars's flanks, obliging him to weaken his center, which would then fold after cavalry charges. After prayers at 3 AM the battle opened with an artillery bombardment at 7:30 AM, but Marlborough's plan quickly encountered severe trouble. The attacks on the French right, launched by the Prince of Orange's Dutch infantry and Scottish Highlanders in the Dutch service, were decimated by French enfilading artillery fire and fierce fighting around the small Tiry Wood in the center of

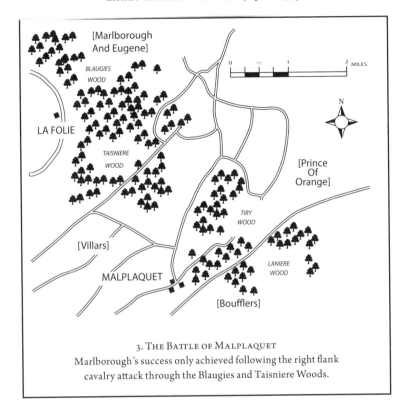

3. The Battle of Malplaquet
Marlborough's success only achieved following the right flank
cavalry attack through the Blaugies and Taisinere Woods.

the gap. Marlborough's plan also failed in its second objective—that
of weakening French resistance to the more important attack on the
French left. There the infantry's progress through the dense Taisinière
Forest was very slow amid fallen tree trunks, some of which had been
used to form abattis, and entrenchments that the French had hurriedly
prepared. Marlborough had planned to attack the forest from two directions, one on the northern side under the leadership of Prince Eugène
and the other from the central gap under his own guidance. Because of
the overgrowth of trees, however, the two attacks could not be coordinated. The resolute French defense, using the trees as concealment, suddenly emerged to fire upon the Danes, Saxons, Hessians, and an English
Guards battalion as they tried to enter and clear the wood. Fighting was
tree by tree, one yard at a time; the wood was cleared only after midday
and at a very heavy cost in lives. The fighting in the center was met with
the same French resolution, and Marlborough's eventual bloody victory

was only assured by an Allied cavalry right flank march around, and concealed by, the Taisinière Forest, threatening the French left and rear at La Folie. Villars reacted as Marlborough had anticipated: he weakened his center in an effort to stabilize his left flank, and in the resulting cavalry melee of sabers in the center, the French were slowly forced to withdraw. The Alliance casualties amounted to twenty-four thousand killed or wounded, and the French to the lesser total of fifteen thousand. Marlborough was able to take Mons, but the casualties, exhaustion, and political factors ended the prospect of an advance on Paris.

THEORETICAL WRITING: COUNT TURPIN DE CRISSÉ

The French military officer and analyst Count Turpin de Crissé, in an exhaustive work titled *Essai sur l'art de la guerre,* addressed personally to King Louis XV, summarized the experiences he gained in warfare.[3] The volume, imprinted with the words "avec approbation et privilèges du roi," was published in 1754, although de Crissé draws considerably on earlier warfare in the sixteenth and seventeenth centuries, covering all aspects of campaigning. Only those aspects dealing with woods and forests, however, are summarized here. De Crissé, born in 1716, was a cavalry officer who fought in seventeen campaigns, ending his career as a lieutenant-general in 1780. As an aristocrat he was forced to flee the country after the French Revolution, and he died in Germany in 1792. To claim that he is a French Clausewitz may be an overstatement, but he certainly deserves to be better known.

Throughout *Essai sur l'art de la guerre* much emphasis is given to the leadership qualities and professional skills required for battle in any terrain. Some of these are timeless; indeed, many later field commanders would have benefited from a greater awareness of these qualities and skills. With regard to forests, de Crissé's first point regards the importance of skilled, trained reconnaissance to determine which woods can or cannot be traversed, as well as warnings on the dubious reliability of maps.

For reconnaissance work, de Crissé prescribes the use of hussars. The first regiment of hussars, who were Hungarian in origin, was formed by Louis XIV in 1692; other army units were often irregulars until the following century. As light cavalry, hussars were charged with the tasks of patrolling, skirmishing, and raiding. De Crissé notes that in most woods there are small clearings that can be used to tactical advantage either for attack or defense. He felt that hussars, in particular, should penetrate woods and clear the way for infantry to follow; the advice of a local guide, if reliable, should be sought and sites for potential enemy ambushes noted. In any night march, columns should follow closely after one another to avoid losing cohesion. De Crissé even suggests that if a column proceeding through a wood or forest is under enemy observation but not under attack, it should advance, retire concealed, and then return again to march, thus giving the enemy an exaggerated impression of its strength—in modern terms, a "force multiplier." All defense positions in woods should have a planned withdrawal route. In the same way as in an advance, in any withdrawal or retreat through forests hussars, wherever possible, should provide a forward and rear guard, protection for the main body, and patrols on the flanks; such arrangements would secure the infantry against flank attacks and ambushes by enemy hussars. An exception might be a forest with trees that are widely spread, where infantry might mount its own flank guards by means of platoons thirty paces on either side of the main columns. Spirited hussar skirmishes could, on occasion, conceal a numerical inferiority.

In an especially noteworthy section, de Crissé offers guidance on small-scale ambushes prepared in woods, which, he argues, are essentially an infantry task. Woods, along with brushwood terrain, vineyards, and low hills, provide opportunities, although proper concealment is always the decisive factor. The move to the ambush site must be accomplished in silence, with soldiers advancing quietly. Dogs should never accompany an ambush, lest they bark; similarly horses might neigh or whinny. If a local *paysan*, drawn by such a noise, should stumble upon the ambush and it appears that, either out of sympathy or the hope of a financial reward, he might reveal this to the enemy, he must quickly be arrested, tied to a tree, and guarded by sentinels. Soldiers in the ambush detachment must be warned that the light of a smoker's pipe can give the ambush away to an enemy patrol; even wind can convey the smell of tobacco. There must be absolutely no noise, either from voices or equipment. If there are to be horses on the ambush site, a rear detachment of hussars should follow with branches attached to the horses' tails to obliterate any sign of hoof marks on the paths; the path's entrance to the wood must also be covered over. If the wood is large, different paths of entry should be chosen to reduce the chance of detection. If the path of entry is long, a section of the ambush party might bypass the ambush site in the hope that an enemy in pursuit would pass the actual site and then, in a surprise attack, be caught from the rear. Sentinels should always be posted along all routes so that they can slip back and inform the main ambush party of an approaching enemy.

De Crissé concludes his counsel on small-scale ambushes with words for the ambush detachment commander. Before any action on the ground, the area must be thoroughly patrolled to ensure that the commander's preparations for the ambush were not observed. A small decoy ambush might even be mounted elsewhere in the area to delude the enemy into thinking that, once this was disposed of, the area was clear and no special security procedures were needed. Finally, the ambush commander must always remain calm in the event of any hitches. If the ambush has been well prepared but his detachment is nevertheless defeated, he need not reproach himself. He must also bear in mind, however, that the pursuit of personal glory, as well as bad judgment, can hand the victory to a superior enemy force.

De Crissé devotes less attention to larger formations concealed in a forest preparing for a surprise attack. Generals should be aware that the enemy's advance guard will be some distance ahead of the concealed main body. This advance guard should be harassed by hussars and other cavalry, who should then withdraw slowly to make the enemy believe that they were only on reconnaissance. Once having drawn the advance guard away from the enemy's main body, the attacker's main body should rush out of the wood with their bayonets, catching their opponents by surprise. At the same time they should turn to attack the enemy's advance guard, with the support of artillery bombardment. The enemy, by now thoroughly confused, would choose to attack the guns, thus giving the infantry its chance to bring about a complete victory.

The Eighteenth Century
New Irregular Challenges

THE EIGHTY YEARS BETWEEN the ending of the War of Spanish Succession and the Napoleonic Wars were to see a slow but steady growth in combat between bodies of men not formed in lines or columns but scouting, skirmishing, harassing, or fighting, often in or from woods and forests. In the major European wars—the War of Austrian Succession, that part of the Seven Years War fought in Europe, the French Revolution and the subsequent Napoleonic Wars—the major engagements still essentially followed traditional patterns by using forests to their advantage on a battlefield; the art of harassing armies by irregulars from the flanks either in battle or on the march grew. Even the greatest field commander of the era, Frederick the Great, King of Prussia, found his armies harassed, and later in life, in response, formed his first Jäger units. In North America, however, forest combat was opening whole new chapters in the history of warfare. Finally, at the end of the era, irregular and semi-irregular combatants operating from forests in Russia played a lead, arguably *the* lead, role in the destruction of one of the largest military forces up to that time assembled in European history, Napoleon's *Grande Armée*.

LIGHT REGIMENTS

These units took a variety of forms, from armed bands of irregular North American Indians and Cossacks to regular Jäger, Chasseurs, Tirailleurs, Light Infantry, and Riflemen.[1] For all these units, the basic infantry soldier's weapon, the musket with its long barrel, stock, and ramrod needed for reloading, was clumsy and totally unsuitable. For units that became regular or semi-regular, functional uniforms had to be made. Tactics and logistics supply procedures had to be thought through. From a slow beginning radical changes were in place by the end of the century, and improvements in training and equipment incorporated lessons learned.

HOCHKIRCH AND TORGAU

Before these major eighteenth-century changes, however, Frederick's campaigns provide two clear cases where forests on the battlefield featured significantly—one a reverse for Frederick, the second a victory.[2]

At Hochkirch, in Saxony, on 14 October 1758, the Austrian commander Marshal Gottfried Daun surprised the Prussians with a dawn attack on Frederick's right flank. Two long columns of infantry moved through pine woods on the slopes of the Kuppritzer Ridge in early morning to turn the Prussians' left, a surprise that led to a sharp reverse for the Prussians. Frederick's army of thirty thousand suffered casualties totaling 9,097, and the Austrian force of thirty-five thousand lost the lesser number of 7,587 men.

The second battle, at Torgau on the middle Elbe, was fought on 3 November 1760. Frederick's army of forty-five thousand was again inferior to Daun's fifty thousand Austrians who also had an overall superiority in artillery, although Frederick had a greater number of the heavier pieces. The Prussian king divided his army in two, Frederick himself leading the larger part in three columns through some twelve miles of wooded country to mount a surprise attack from Elsnig on a low ridge on the northern flank of the Austrian position. At the same time the smaller force prepared an attack upon the stiffer slopes of the southern flank near Suptitz. Coordination of the twenty-four thousand infantry and six thousand cavalry in the northern flank's wooded conditions proved very difficult, with abattis, forester guides providing misleading directions, and the trees all making the passage of the artillery slow. Frederick's attacks, consequently, were carried out piecemeal, not at all as he had planned, and he suffered heavy casualties. Victory for the

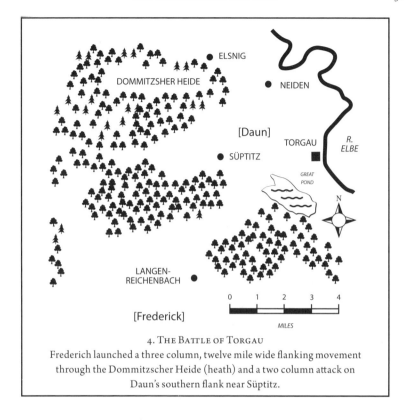

4. THE BATTLE OF TORGAU

Frederich launched a three column, twelve mile wide flanking movement
through the Dommitzscher Heide (heath) and a two column attack on
Daun's southern flank near Süptitz.

Prussians was, however, secured by the attack on the Austrian southern flank. To conceal movement from the Austrians for as long as possible, and also to move around the left of the Austrian position as far as
possible, this attack force also rode along forest paths but with greater
success. The victory was costly, the total casualties for the Prussians at
least sixteen thousand, perhaps as many as twenty thousand, considerably more than the fifteen thousand Austrians killed or wounded. Both
army commanders were hit—Daun was wounded but Frederick only
had his clothing torn. Nevertheless, the battle resulted in the Prussians
regaining control of Saxony.

Heavy infantry column and line tactics generally dominated the
fields of battle. Flank movements requiring long preliminary marches
by ill-led men were thought to be fatiguing, especially through forests. Commanders were well aware of the problems for musketeers and

artillery men in woods. Additionally, any movement of guns inside a forest involved time-consuming hacking to create some form of path through the trees and their roots. Concepts of any form of light infantry were still limited to skirmishing, where the very small bodies of men involved were not a viable target to annihilating cavalry charges. Woods were seen as useful for concealment if the terrain so permitted. Entry into a wood was to be avoided; the only justifiable exception was as a route to secure a surprise but certainly not as a battlefield. Frederick also generally avoided issuing orders for a march through woods, as such marches provided opportunities for soldiers to desert.

Guerrillas or partisans of the period occasionally lived in forests and quite often used woods to conceal their movements before or after attack. The best were the Croatians and Hungarians in the Austrian Army that continually harassed the Prussians. There were also other "freedom fighters" with arms usually limited to sporting weapons. Late in his life, in 1783, Frederick ordered the formation of three units of *Frei-Regimenter,* intended primarily to head any advance and engage the enemy in close combat but another role was to occupy woodlands.[3]

NORTH AMERICA: MONONGAHELA

Events on the other side of the Atlantic, where North American forests were far more abundant, had already forced the British Army to urgently reappraise their positions in three wars: the French and Indian War of 1754–56, the Seven Years War of 1756–63, and America's War of Independence of 1775–83. The scale of the battles was miniscule compared to the scale of those in Europe, but in any history of forest warfare, and for infantry history in particular, they were of greater significance. Both the actions and the lessons learned merit recording in some detail.

The British learning curve began in the first of the three wars in 1754, a sharp conflict between the thirteen British seaboard colonies in North America and French colonists assisted by indigenous "Indians." The area of the British colonies extended from Newfoundland southward to Georgia and were peopled by various settled communities. The area settled by the French was largely limited to Quebec, Montreal, and the St. Lawrence Valley with "Acadia" (now Nova Scotia and a part of New Brunswick) in the north together with Louisiana in the south. The French wanted to penetrate a wide area of hinterland territory that could link the two areas and had built a chain of timber forts with swivel guns to contain any British expansion. For this purpose they had also secured the support of local Indian communities and constructed a number of forts south of Lake Erie heading toward the Ohio River. In early 1754 the French robustly forced the withdrawal of a force of British colonists led by Lieutenant-Colonel George Washington that had been ordered to support the building of a fort to assert British control of the area; the French, however, had arrived first and were building Fort Duquesne—on the site of the modern city of Pittsburgh. In reply, London dispatched a force of two British Army Line Infantry regiments under the command of Major-General Edward Braddock with orders to occupy the Ohio Valley area. The regiments were fully trained in the military warfare tactics of Frederick the Great, shooting in ranks from traditional squares and moving in columns. They were to meet the tactics of Frederick's German forbear, Arminius, developed by the French and the Indians, to a fine operational art after the battle of the Monongahela River on 8 July 1755.

Braddock assembled his force, strengthened by a detachment of light cavalry and artillery together with militias from the North American colonies at Fort Cumberland. Lieutenant-Colonel Washington joined the force as Braddock's aide-de-camp. The British units had only rudimentary forest training, and the American militia contingents had very little military training of any type, with the exception of the Virginians. On the march the columns had to be accompanied by a long baggage train, a few nurses and wives, and other followers. Maps were very general, lacking most useful topographical detail. The terrain to be covered between Fort Cumberland and Duquesne was that of hills, mountains, and endless thick forest with no roads and few tracks. These conditions were ideally suited to the French Canadian militiamen and the war-painted Indians, both well experienced in forests, with the additional advantage of having access to a water supply from the local river systems. The one thousand or so French regulars, the French Canadians, and many of their Indian allies in the area were equipped with the light Tulle muskets, the Indians also carrying knives and tomahawks for the

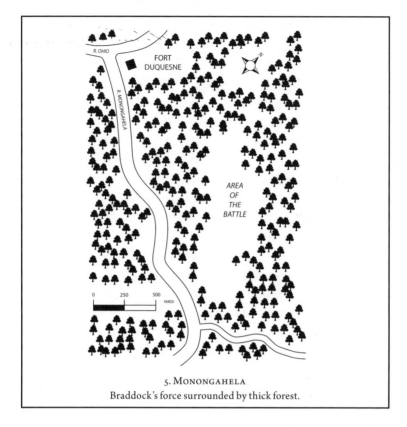

5. MONONGAHELA
Braddock's force surrounded by thick forest.

all-important scalping of opponents. The length of the clumsy "Brown
Bess" musket and the risk that if the powder in the priming pan became
moist the gun would not fire were severe disadvantages in the damp forest conditions. Most officers preferred to use trained soldiers for bayonet
charges, but charges were not possible in forest conditions.

Braddock's advance was slow, limited to narrow, twisted, and rough
tracks, around and over thickly forested hills. He had to use carpenters
to make a road for his guns, and for the two hundred supply wagons
and their several hundred horses. Some hills were so steep that the light
American draught horses were not equal to the task, and a system of
block and tackle was needed for hauling the guns. European-style for-
aging for food and fodder was totally impossible, and therefore supply
wagons and cattle for slaughter could not be left far behind; some had
to be up front. The column started at no more than two miles a day, but

later, after some reorganization, it reached an average of three to three and three-quarter miles. Bullocks had proved particularly difficult to control in forest conditions.

The lead detachment was comprised of the two British Line regiments, some of the American militia companies, the carpenters, and some sailors and artillerymen, with the Virginian scouts at their head. Following some distance behind was the second detachment, with more guns, stores, ammunition, and a few wives, children, and camp followers. Most of the latter, however, were traveling in unsuitable heavy wagons, characteristic of European warfare, and soon were ordered to return to Fort Cumberland. Both detachments, which formed a column that often extended more than four miles along a narrow track, were uncomfortably aware that Canadians and Indians, concealed in the woods aligning the track, were watching their progress. A few local clashes erupted, but the dense nature of the forest and hills led Braddock to decide not to send out a sufficient number of flank scouts, which was a fatal mistake. The initiative lay with the French.

A historian of the 44th Foot, one of two British Line regiments, described the march:

> A strange enough site in those wild woods must have been the long train of jolting waggons, dragged by ill-conditioned horses, growing daily weaker; the clumsy tumbrils and artillery and ammunition carts jolting and crashing over the rough-made track; the strings of heavily laden packhorses stung by deerflies and goaded by drivers' whips, sliding and slipping over limestone slabs and floundering amid stumps and roots; the droves of stunted cattle shambling unwillingly along the unfenced track; the fresh-faced soldiers, in tight scarlet uniforms, pigtails and pipe clay, mitre hats and white-gaitered legs, sweltering in the fierce, unwanted heat of an American mid-summer sun.[4]

Of a later one-hundred-mile advance on Fort Duquesne another historian wrote that the track construction work involved "hewing, digging, blasting, laying gabions to support the track along the sides of steep declivities."[5]

Braddock aimed to take Fort Duquesne with the lead detachment before the arrival of French reinforcements, which he knew to be on their way. The fort's garrison, under its commander Daniel de Beaujeu, was a much inferior force, some nine hundred regular naval infantrymen but no artillery. De Beaujeu, after consulting with his predecessor who was still in the fort, decided that Braddock must be attacked while on the move, before he could besiege and bombard the fort into submission. Accordingly, on the morning of 9 July 1755, de Beaujeu led a party of the garrison out, soon encountering Braddock's advance guard in the forest near the right bank of the Monongahela, ten miles away from the fort.[6]

Under fire from within the forest, the British redcoats immediately formed two lines, one kneeling, one standing, and both shouting "God Save the King," they fired back into the trees; two six-pounder guns were brought up to support their volleys. The attack was repelled, de Beaujeu was killed, and Braddock gained a short-lived success. De Beaujeu's successor, Jean-Daniel Dumas, rallied the supporting French Canadians together with some six hundred Indians who moved into the forest on either side of the British column. They quickly disposed of the weak flank scouts and then opened a murderous fire into the British ranks, the Indians' war cries adding an unnerving racket. Confusion spread as men fell and the advance guard retreated back into the main body. The very large trees of the wood offered perfect cover for the attackers, running swiftly from behind one tree to another. But they provided no fixed targets for the encircled British, blinded by smoke and trained just for squares and synchronized volleys. Only the Virginians attempted to emulate the Indians by moving into the trees and using them as cover, but Braddock, at the point of his sword, ordered them back. Officers were priority targets for the French and Indians, with their deaths increasing the chaos. The soldiers closed ranks, thus providing even better targets. The Indians had only to fire into the ranks; specific aiming was unnecessary. Small group charges by the British infantry were quickly shot down. Redcoats fell in scores.

The slaughter was followed by scalping and other ritual tortures for the men captured. The forward detachment commander was killed; Braddock himself was wounded and died the following day. Washington, the commanding officer of one of the line regiments, and a few other surviving officers rallied, gathered survivors together, and retreated to the Monongahela. They crossed the river in considerable disorder and fell back toward the second detachment in an evening and night march.

Fig. 4.1. The French and Indian attack on General Braddock's column, Monongahela.
(Courtesy of the Wisconsin Historical Society, Image ID 1900)

The track was strewn with wounded and dying crying out for help. The darkness of the forest on either side of the track added to the gloom of the defeat. Survivors reached the second detachment over the next two days; the detachment then withdrew to the safety of Fort Cumberland. Sixty-three out of the eighty-nine British Army officers had been killed; fewer than five hundred out of the thirteen hundred rank and file survived. All the guns and wagons were lost. A short while later a second smaller column was attacked, but on this occasion the regulars stood firm, avoiding panic.

The battle, small scale in terms of the numbers involved, was nevertheless to have profound theoretical and practical consequences. The danger of this form of forest warfare was graphically described in an anonymous contemporary writer's impressions of an earlier expedition in Ohio territory. This expedition seems to have been primarily a reconnaissance.[7]

> Let us suppose a person, who is entirely unacquainted with the nature of this service to be put at the head of an expedition in America. We will further suppose that he had made the dispositions usual in Europe for a march, or to receive an enemy; and that he is then attacked by the savages. He cannot discover them, tho' from every tree, log or bush he receives an incessant fire and observes that few of their shots are lost. He will not hesitate to charge these enemies but he will charge in vain. For they are as cautious to avoid a close engagement, as indefatigable in harrassing his troops and notwithstanding all his endeavour he will still find himself surrounded by a circle of fire, which, like an artificial horizon, follows him everywhere.
>
> Unable to rid himself of an enemy who never stands his attacks, and flies when pressed, only to return upon him again with equal agility and vigour; he will see the courage of his heavy troop droop, and their strength at last fail them by repeated and ineffective efforts.
>
> He must therefore think of a retreat, unless he can force his way thro' the enemy. But how is this to be effected? his baggage and provisions are unloaded and scattered, part of his horses and drivers killed, others dispersed by fear, and his wounded to be carried by soldiers already fainting under the fatigue of a long action. The enemy, encouraged by his distress, will not fail to increase the disorder, by pressing upon him by every side, with redoubled fury and savage howlings.
>
> He will probably form a circle or a square, to keep off so daring an enemy ready at the least opening to fall upon him with the destructive tomahawk; but these dispositions, tho' a tolerable shift for defence, are neither proper for an attack, nor a march thro' the woods.

The Monongahela disaster was analyzed by a perceptive and professional Swiss soldier, Henry Bouquet, from his own experience. He argued that combat in such conditions required units lightly equipped and armed, the abandonment of close order column and square tactics, and rapid pursuit into the forests giving no time for the enemy to rally. When log forts were built in forest areas, the ground surrounding them was to be cleared and trees felled to force the attackers out into the open. Later, all attackers would themselves clear ground around a fort for artillery gun positions.

HENRY BOUQUET

The commander-in-chief of the British Army, William, Duke of Cumberland, had drawn the same conclusions from Braddock's defeat, and he accepted a proposal from another Swiss soldier, Jacques Prevost, at the time serving in Holland under the Prince of Orange. The proposal was for the formation of two specially trained corps, eventually four battalions each of ten companies. It was put into effect by General Lord Loudoun, the British commander in North America. Bouquet and a third Swiss officer, Haldimand, were appointed to command the 1st and 2nd Battalions of the I Corps formally raised in March 1756 as the Royal American Regiment—the term "Royal" to give it prestige and "American" to indicate clearly that it was created for one theater of operations only.[8]

The Royal American Regiment was very different from the British Army's Line Redcoats.[9] After special legislation the battalions were permitted to recruit fifty foreign officers: they had to be Protestant, could only serve in America, and could not be promoted beyond the rank of lieutenant-colonel. In reality, however, a high proportion of the first officers of the four battalions were Scots, a few were Swiss, German, and Dutch, and the remainder were English or Irish. Other foreign officers were also permitted in a linked special woodland engineer regiment. Many of the battalions' soldiers were of Swiss, Tyrolean, or German origin who had settled in America.

The traditional redcoat was replaced by a brown cloth jacket, shirt, leggings, trousers, a soft cap, and a *surtout* cape coated with two layers of oil to keep out the rain as well as a green additive, when possible, for protective coloring.

A second corps on the same pattern, a short-lived 80th Foot, was also raised in America in 1757. It was much smaller, comprising only one battalion of five companies, and was disbanded at the end of the Seven Years' War.[10]

In addition to the Royal American Regiment and the 80th Foot, Line infantry battalions were restructured to include a Light company tasked to pursue and engage enemies in rough country and forests, and a Grenadier company to form one of the two flank guards of a column for a march on a narrow track. In training, special emphasis was placed on accurate shooting, and soldiers were issued a dark-blue tunic with no lace but with extra pockets for ammunition. Very soon afterward the Light companies of Line battalions were grouped together in Light Infantry battalions. For his own operation, Bouquet recruited special bodies of men: hunters, flankers, and scouts. Bouquet wrote careful, to use the modern term, "standard operational procedures" for fighting among trees. These writings and precepts are instructive, providing evidence not only of his experience and clear thinking on forest warfare but also illustrating the details needed for such operations in this period. His own recruited men—particularly the five-hundred-strong battalions of Hunters—had to be in shape to carry their equipment, walk and run well, jump over logs and ditches, swim pushing a raft with their clothing and equipment before them, and advance at the run in extended order wheeling in on the flanks of their opponents. Skill at arms requirements included the ability to fire at a rapid rate while standing, kneeling, or lying on the ground. Hunter soldiers also had to learn how to prepare for battle, live in forests, dig entrenchments, make fascines, fell trees, saw planks, and construct canoes, wagons, carts, bridges, ovens, small forts, and log houses. Attached Light Horse troops required similar training as well as training in the use of a battleax. Their horsemanship had to include rapid mounting and dismounting, galloping through woods, and jumping ditches and obstructions; their horses had to be trained to swim. In addition, and presumably only if available, a bloodhound was to accompany each mounted trooper to detect ambushes and to follow tracks.[11]

Bouquet also set out battlefield procedures recommending that no force in forest warfare should in total number more than 1,800, two Line or a Royal American battalions each of 500, a Hunter battalion of 500, two 50-man troops of Light Horse , a small 20-strong company of artillery, and no more than 250 drivers and other support personnel. The daily ration for all would be a pound and a half of meat and a pound of flour with a gill of salt per week. For the transport of tools, food, and ammunition, either 731 horses or 640 oxen, if affordable and available, would pull the wagons or carts. Encampments were to be in the form of a parallelogram, the term "square" still being used, with the Line infantry on all four sides; the Light Horse battalion in the center; and the Hunters in redoubts at each angle, two each on the long sides of the parallelogram and one more at the front and at the rear, each with twenty-two men and seven sentries.

In an advance march, the force convoy had to be preceded by small scouting parties searching for ambushes in the forest in front and on the flanks, with hunters covering the work of the artificers and axmen needed to cut the road. These scouting parties would be followed by the force convoy in the shape of a parallelogram or rectangle, fourteen hundred yards long. At the head of this new type of "square" there were to be 150 regular infantrymen in double file; 250 infantrymen were to march in single file on each of the long sides of the square, with the Light Horse battalion inside it. Following them were to be two additional detachments of infantrymen, 150 and 100 strong in double file, hunters in two files, the Light Horse battalion, the wagons, stores and cattle, and the convoy's Rear Guard of hunters. Throughout the march through wooded areas, flankers would continue to patrol the woods along the entire length of the convoy's flanks.

If the convoy had to enter a defile, hunters with their bloodhounds would be the first to reconnoiter and then occupy the heights, the center and right flank columns would enter the defile next, followed by the wagons and cattle, the flank files, the Light Horse troops, the two center rear parties and the rear guard.

The additional instructions set out by Bouquet cover defense within and attacks mounted from the diamond-shaped parallelogram encampments but appear to be based on combat in more open terrain; at the same time he notes the speed of movement that the specially trained units could provide to encircle groups of attackers. While Bouquet's teachings on training, encampments, and marching convoys undoubtedly provided useful advice and guidance for field commanders, it is most unlikely that they were always followed to the letter. Their importance lies in their detailed account of the earliest British Army doctrine on fighting in woods and forests.[12]

NORTH AMERICA, 1756–83

In May 1756 the Seven Years' War opened, involving increasing numbers of British and French regular units as well as French Canadians and Indians. The major engagements were not fought in thick forested areas but both armies used forests in their planning, either for the launching of surprise attacks on forts or to try to channel their opponents to ground of their own choosing. At the same time, in small-scale, low-intensity warfare consisting of ambushes, lightning raids, and skirmishes, forest-based tactics were used by both sides even, and particularly, in the winter months. The French continued to use French Canadians and Indians for this *petite guerre* warfare; the British used informal locally raised parties of Rangers, notably those of Major Robert Rogers, as well as the Light companies of Line Infantry battalions, some now issued with carbines and, in winter, snowshoes. These were used on scouting tasks and for protecting supply columns. The most important purely forest operations took place after the May 1763 Treaty of Paris that ended the war with France. But later in the year the British were faced with a final reckoning with the Indians. In the first operation Colonel Bouquet, at the head of a column of some five hundred including companies of the 42nd Infantry and the Royal American Regiment, was marching to relieve Fort Pitt. The heat and dryness of early August made for very difficult forest conditions. Near a low hill known as Bushy Run, Bouquet's small column came under fire from Pontiac Indians, who first fired at the head of the column and then moved among trees to fire at the flank, finally encircling it. The column suffered severe casualties. Bouquet retained order, however, and instructed his infantry to form a defensive "square" facing outward and to fire at their attackers. The battle raged for most of the day, 5 August, with the "square" turning into a defensive encampment for the night. The Indians, screeching and yelling, made repeated mass attacks in the early morning, and the column's situation became critical. Bouquet then decided to open up the encampment's circle to form a trap, with the right flank concealed among trees. The Indians poured into the gap, only to be cut down by troops firing from behind the trees. A follow-up bayonet charge completed their rout, and Bouquet duly reached Fort Pitt.

The second operation followed in early October, a month before Bouquet was ordered home. His column now totaled more than fifteen hundred. It had been reinforced by three parties of Virginians and two military units from Pennsylvania, but, out of necessity, it also included a large logistic component of sheep, cattle, and packhorses carrying provisions with the necessary staffs, including women nurses. The Virginians formed an advance scouting group in three parties some distance in front and on either flank, establishing three clear parallel paths. Next came carpenter pioneers with an escort of light infantry, also divided into three parties, one for each path and all under the column's chief engineer. Then followed the main body with all the wagons and livestock in the center, escorted at the front by men from the 42nd, on the left by a battalion of Pennsylvanians, and on the right by the Royal Americans. The second Pennsylvanian unit formed the rear guard. The men marched in extended order two yards apart, in total silence, with orders to form a "square" and face outward if attacked.[13] The thick forest gloom, oozing black soil, and decaying fallen trees were particularly challenging.

In the end, the casualties suffered by the Indians at Bushy Run and the by now impressive strength and tactics of the British led the Indians to seek peace at a large assembly at Muskingum a month later. Bouquet, who had taken on British nationality, was promoted to brigadier-general upon the recommendation of both Houses of Parliament. He died suddenly from fever and exhaustion in 1765.

The last eighteenth-century war in North America, America's War of Independence in 1775–82, was fought mainly but not entirely by larger formations of men than fought in the Seven Years' War, and also in terrain more familiar to the British and their German regiments—slightly wooded or open country, farmlands, plantations, grasslands, villages, and towns. Woods for flank attacks and ambushes were frequently used by both sides in planning a battle, notably at Saratoga in 1772 and Guilford Court House in 1781. In several regions, swamps covered with high bushes provided special opportunities. Trees were felled to block tracks or roads, to build forts or strongholds, or to divert streams to flood particular areas into a swamp.[14] American marksmen snipers would conceal themselves in tall trees and pick off British officers, and, in reply, British artillerymen would rake a wood with canister case shot. British regiments on the march through country interspersed with woods would put out flank guards. American units used woods for winter quarters, occasionally to emerge for a hit-and-run attack. In a few areas of South Carolina the swamps and forests were linked, with trees growing in several inches of water. These came to provide doubly secure assembly areas for irregular or semi-regular militia guerrilla detachments, notably those of "Swamp Fox" Francis Marion, Andrew Pickens, and Thomas Sumter, to prepare for a raid.

The most striking example of a forest battle, small scale but dramatic, occurred on 7 October 1780 when a detachment of General Charles Cornwallis's army marching toward North Carolina from South Carolina was so severely harassed by American militias that it unwisely retreated to the peak hill of a sixteen-mile-long range of hills known as Kings Mountain. Although the peak was bare, tall pines reached from the base of the range to very near the top. Cornwallis's detachment, thirteen hundred strong, included a hundred men from loyalist American units together with a thousand less well-trained militia all led by Major Patrick Ferguson, the only British officer present, who feared encirclement. Their opponents were mounted frontiersmen each with their own group leader drawn from a number of regions of the two Carolinas, western Virginia, and Tennessee, all in a very loose organization. They rode to the base of the forest where they dismounted and attempted to carry the peak by frontal advance and charge but were stopped or shot down by Ferguson's men. Ferguson then, in a rash move, ordered his men to charge down the hillside. The Americans, taking cover behind the trees, simply picked off their opponents as they charged repeatedly. One thousand men of the loyalist contingent were killed, wounded, or captured, including Ferguson himself who was killed when he refused to surrender; only twenty-eight Americans lost their lives.[15] An important contribution to the American success was their use of a muzzle-loaded rifle, while the nature of the battle highlighted the obvious unsuitability of the "Brown Bess." The defeat and other difficulties obliged Cornwallis

Fig. 4.2. The Death of Cornet Geary at Flemington, New Jersey, in 1776.
(Monument in St. Nicholas Church, Great Bookham, Surrey, England)

to abandon his 1780 invasion of North Carolina, a significant step toward the ultimate defeat of the British.

EUROPEAN PEASANT UPRISINGS

The turn of the eighteenth and nineteenth centuries saw two regional peasant uprisings in Europe in which insurgents with mixed political and also regrettably criminal motives struck out from and took refuge in forest or wood hideouts. These were the 1794–96 Chouan uprising in France and the 1809 Tyrolean revolt; "Anno Neun."

The Chouans were a minority in revolt against the French revolutionary anti-Christian Directorate government; they operated in rural and wooded areas north of the Loire and Brittany.[16] They briefly controlled both Nantes and Le Mans and were led by a saddle maker, Jean

Cottereau, who changed his name to Jean Chouan, derived from the sound made by long-eared owls, a sound the rebels imitated when calling to one another. They preferred to stage surprise attacks at night and wore a distinctive style of dress—peasant breeches, short jackets, and a round hat. General Hoche, using mobile pursuit groups, quelled the uprising in 1796, although small bands operated for another four years.

The Tyrol revolt, led by an innkeeper named Andres Hofer, was a rebellion of Austrians against a French-supported Bavarian occupation.[17] Hofer's followers, several thousand strong, included some from the local militia bearing firearms but others carrying only scythes or clubs. Engagements were fought on open ground, on forest edges, or in villages. When pursued, the insurgents would retreat up the steep tree-covered mountainsides; on at least one occasion, from there they rolled down tree trunks or boulders, their speed accelerating, to topple their pursuers, an unusual and frightening variant of forest warfare. Although the insurgents entered Innsbruck three times, the Bavarians, with help from the French, soon put down the uprising.

THE NAPOLEONIC WARS: BARROSA

The campaign of Arthur Wellesley, Duke of Wellington, in the Iberian Peninsula was fought mainly around or in cities, or in gorse, heather, or other scrub or rocky terrain. Battle plans took into account the need to avoid olive groves, copses, and small woods. The principal use of spinneys and copses appears to have been for the purpose of gathering intelligence. Small light cavalry patrols would hide in a copse and observe, and count, the movements and size of their opponent's forces crossing a bridge or passing through a valley. Others would collect general topographical information.

One important battle that did involve woods was the Battle of Barrosa in southern Spain on 5 March 1811.[18] The battle was fought as part of an attempt to relieve the Spanish and British garrison holding Cadiz against a twenty-five-thousand-strong French siege force commanded by Marshal Claude Victor. The attempt was to be a combination of a sortie by the garrisons and an attack from the east following landings on the coast by two Spanish divisions and two British brigades, all to

6. THE BATTLE OF BARROSA
Two British brigades fight through a pine forest
to attack two French divisons on Barrosa Hill and Ridge.

be commanded by the Spanish general Manuel la Peña. The operation met with coordination difficulties, delays, and fatigue following
the approach marches. On the morning of the 5th, la Peña ordered the
Spanish formations to advance westward along the coastal road toward
Cadiz and, simultaneously, the British brigades to advance on the south
to north Barossa Ridge in order to prepare for a right flank attack on
French lines of communication. The slopes leading to the summit of
the ridge were covered in pine woods, particularly at the bottom. The
two brigades, along with Portuguese flank companies, marched down
the slopes only to learn that two French divisions in a wide sweep had
turned their own flank and rear behind the Barossa Ridge and were
threatening the coastal road. The weary soldiers were then ordered to
head back through the woods to oppose the French. Their vigorous
commander, General Sir Thomas Graham, then ordered each brigade,

despite their numerical inferiority, to attack one of the two French divisions. The French were taken totally by surprise.

The fighting in the woods, on both the western and eastern sides of the ridge, was close combat, at times hand to hand. Two battalions were sent on ahead in skirmishing order, and the rest followed in two lines. Accounts of the battle suggest that the noise of battle was unusual in both volume and form as men darted for cover among trees on the slopes, attempting to maintain some order in the one or two lines of advance. Added to the usual noise of musketry and French artillery, the cries of the wounded, and shouted orders, there was a chorus of cheers—the Portuguese shouting "Que bella musica," the Irish 87th Foot calling out "Faugh au Ballagh" (Clear the way), and an English battalion scrambling through the pines yelling "Hearts of Oak." French regiments at this time were known to attack to chants of "La Marseillaise" or the revolutionary song "Ca ira," and, although it is not recorded in English accounts of this particular battle, the French are likely to have done so at Barossa. The colonel of one of the skirmishing battalions was heard shouting, "Fire at their legs and spoil their dancing." The battle lasted several hours. In the end the British and Portuguese had defeated a French force nearly twice their size, and the 87th had captured the eagle standard of a French regiment. The French were forced to withdraw, but la Peña failed to follow up on this victory.

THE NAPOLEONIC WARS: RUSSIA, 1812–13

Woods and forests played an important part in Napoleon's 1812 invasions of Russia and its catastrophic outcome. In planning for the campaign Napoleon had studied books on Russia's geographical conditions, but convinced that he would lead a victorious three-month-long campaign, he took no particular note.[19] However, a month and a day after the start of the invasion, on 25 July, the *Grande Armée* learned its first lesson about Russia's vast forests following a cavalry charge near Ostrovno. Joachim Murat's cavalry captured a Russian battery, but the Russian force retired into a wood where the French regiment could not enter. Woods were to further aggravate the glamorously uniformed cavalry, with low branches tearing at helmets and uniform embellishments.

More serious was the narrow width of the Russian roads, most little more than tracks which, even when not reduced to dust or mud from heavy rains, could cause traffic jams in forests; detours or trying to maneuver off the sides of roads which were not passable. As the *Grande Armée* penetrated deeper into Russia, small groups of partisans operating from woods and forests began to harass the army, at first only attacking individual French or Allied soldiers and then small groups.

In late October the *Grande Armée* began its great retreat, now much reduced in numbers following casualties, disease, and desertion, its uniforms hopelessly unsuitable for the advancing winter and with most of the soldiers suffering from malnutrition. Hunger drove many of them to forage, hunt, or pillage, even though, if caught in the woods by Russian peasants, they would be murdered. On the different tracks, and later the Moscow-Smolensk road, the army's columns were harassed by regular mounted Cossack units, some with light artillery, Kuban and Don Cossack irregulars on ponies, and Bashkir horsemen—some twenty thousand in total.[20] Some of the irregular Cossacks had firearms, many had swords, and many more wielded a crude lance or pike in the form of a wooden pole with a pointed metal tip. The Bashkirs still used bows and arrows. The *Grande Armée*'s cavalry, in particular, had suffered in the campaign and could no longer provide flank guards, with the result that its retreating columns were continuously attacked from roadside woods. Perhaps greater than the infliction of any large number of casualties was the effect of these attacks on the morale of the soldiers, already despairing and losing cohesion. Prisoners taken by the Cossacks, if not immediately killed, were treated with the utmost brutality: beaten, denied food and water, and stripped naked in the glacial cold. The large majority of these died later on marches to captivity.

Two small-scale forest battles in the grimmest phase of the retreat merit mention. The first victory was gained by a small body of men, only some two thousand strong, under Marshal Michel Ney. His force was in danger of being cut off, encircled by Russian forces that prevented his crossing the Dnepr River. To confuse his opponents, Ney ordered that a large number of campfires be lit in a wood to give the impression that he was not moving out. He then led his men, amid great difficulty, through woods and rough country to a safer crossing place. The second

success, also Ney's work, occurred during the Berezina crossing operations. Ney was charged by Napoleon to hold off an attack by massive and
well-equipped Russian formations moving to block the last regiment of
the *Grande Armée* waiting its turn to cross the river. Ney's force, despite
its poor condition and led by Polish lancers and Swiss infantry, fought
a daylong battle, mainly in the local conifer forests. The force suffered
heavy casualties, many from tree splinters following Russian artillery
bombardment, but the Russian plan was thwarted.

Returning into Germany, the survivors and newly raised regiments
found that the Cossacks' role had been taken over by the Freikorps
Jägers who maintained a steady momentum of harrying and harassment
launched from woods.

THEORETICAL WRITING: CLAUSEWITZ

The late eighteenth and very early nineteenth centuries saw further
theoretical military writing. Much of it was concerned with the wide
variety of light regiments being formed with skirmishing and scouting
roles.[21] References to specific woods and forest fighting, however, were
marginal. Other writers were more interested in theories of war as a
whole, grand strategies, and the conduct of operations rather than terrain. The great Prussian writer Carl von Clausewitz did, however, offer
some reflections, sparing but forceful.

In *On War* he first emphasized the need for military commanders
to know the nature of any forest, whether dense and impenetrable or
more cultivated with paths.[22] In the case of the more cultivated forests,
he asserted that they were best avoided or at least kept in the rear of
any prepared defense position. Defense positions in the forest itself or
with the trees in front of defenders would render them blind, whereas a
forest in the defenders' rear would not obscure observation and would
also provide a screen behind which the defenders could prepare for any
further movements or withdrawal. Clausewitz saw this as of particular
value in the likely event that the defenders' strength was weak. He was
more positive about the role of dense forests traversed by roads, which
could provide cover for a retreat or used to kill attackers as they emerged
from the forest. Nevertheless, he remained doubtful on the overall value

of forests for combat defense, believing that even the thickest could be infiltrated, resulting in a general breakthrough. He dismissed abattis as having only psychological value. Woods and forests, in his view, were of lesser value than a swamp or river. Based no doubt on his own campaign experience, he concluded that any force attempting to pass through vast forest areas such as those in Poland and Russia at a time of national uprising would be in serious trouble if the maneuver was unsuccessful. Forests presented huge supply problems, especially if the defenders' plans forced the attacker on lines of communication through deep forest. Here superiority in numbers would count for little. For such terrain, both he and the second important military analyst of the period, Henri de Jomini, could only advocate protective skirmishing and patrolling as a defense for lines of communication.

Toward Later Modern Warfare
1815–1914

THE NINETY-NINE YEARS BETWEEN the Congress of Vienna and the outbreak of the First World War in 1914 saw dramatic change in warfare. Mass mobilization could be achieved more swiftly with the development of railways, new and more deadly weapons ranged from the bolt-action rifle and machine guns to heavier artillery, and (with the exception of the French Army) a shift from colorful uniforms to khaki or *feldgrau*. Officers and generals received a more thorough training, however theoretical and at times insufficient, necessitated by unfortunate experiences. At the same time some armies, notably the French, British, and German, learned practical skills in imperial campaigns far from Europe; these skills included adaptability, improvisation, and occasionally forest warfare.

These nine decades saw combat in both Europe and North America in a variety of terrains. The three most important of the era's wars were the American Civil War, the war between Prussia and Austria, and the war between the Prussian-led North German Confederation and France.

THE AMERICAN CIVIL WAR

The American Civil War (1861–65) saw certain changes in operational art from the warfare fifty years earlier. The movement of soldiers over considerable distances had become more efficient and rapid, sometimes by rail but also by inland waterways and improved roads for mule- or horse-drawn wagons. Communication had become more efficient, by semaphore signaling from hilltops and sometimes by telegraph over short distances. But most soldiers of both armies were still equipped with traditional single-shot, muzzle-loading muskets or rifles which one had to stand up to fire in volleys; artillery guns, though often used efficiently, were still of Napoleonic-era design. And both the northern Federal and southern Confederate armies had to hurriedly recruit substantial numbers of men, volunteers, and conscripts who were poorly trained. Not all field commanders were competent, although the generals of both armies, especially the Confederate Army, had the advantage of fighting on home ground with full topographical intelligence, though they did not always draw fully upon it. The Confederates, too, were fighting a defensive war on a very wide front that provided opportunities to attack Federal lines of supply as the Northerners attempted to move south or east. This varied range of factors affected combat tactics, not least in woods and forests.

In general, at this halfway stage between eighteenth- and twentieth-century modern warfare, the tactics of both armies remained the traditional close formation. In open country, infantry advanced in four lines with men two deep and not far apart, and the lines separated by two hundred to seven hundred yards; perhaps because it was a passionate civil war, greater importance was attached to momentum. Cavalry retained its traditional functions with swords when mounted and carbines or revolvers when on foot. The basic artillery weapon was the old flat-trajectory twelve-pounder smooth bore gun, capable of firing solid, shrapnel, explosive, and, to a limited extent, grapeshot rounds at four hundred to five hundred yards. Soldiers in both armies, as a result of poor training, tended to open fire from the moment they saw an opponent rather than await effective range; also, when achieving success, units would neglect the importance of consolidation. Poor light, especially in forests, often made it difficult to distinguish friends from foe, although yells from attacking infantry, such as the Southern "Three times three Tennessee," helped maintain cohesion.[1] Woods and forests presented the usual problems not only of cohesion but also of morale, supplies, food and water, and the wounded and the dead. Artillery could not support a charge and very often could not be moved to positions near to the front in wooded areas.

The American landscape, especially in the eastern seaboard states, had changed greatly since the eighteenth-century wars, with the development of farming, new towns, trading centers and markets, villages, roads, and railways. Much of the Civil War fighting therefore took place in plantations, orchards, fields, and small towns and villages; wooded areas were sparse and did not have the effect on battle as in earlier years. The two major battles that were fought in woods, however, suffered many of the same problems of the past and foreshadowed some to follow in the future. These were the Battle of Chancellorsville in April–May 1863 and the Battle of the Wilderness in May of the following year, both fought in Virginia and over much the same ground.[2]

CHANCELLORSVILLE AND THE WILDERNESS

The first of these two battles, at Chancellorsville, was fought over the Federal attempt to control a road in this area running east to west, from Washington and Fredericksburg to the Confederate capital of Richmond. In December 1862, despite inferior numbers, the Confederates had won an important victory at Fredericksburg. To the south and west of Fredericksburg lay more than sixty-five square miles of thick overgrown wasteland, from the Rapidan River to Spotsylvania, which came to be known to soldiers as "the Wilderness." A region in which trees—pine, oak, and maple—had been cut down for fuel, it was now a huge landscape of tree stumps and tall, thick bush undergrowth with oak and pine saplings growing up to replace the felled trees. In one central area, five miles from Fredericksburg, lay the small trading center of Chancellorsville, with its crossroads cutting through the area's distinctive thick and overgrown heavy woods of living trees, forming the local Chancellorsville Forest. The Rappahannock River ran northwest of Fredericksburg, continuing along the northeastern edge of the forest for just over five miles. The main river then continued northwest; a tributary, the Rapidan, ran along the rest of the northern edge of the forest before its juncture with the Rappahannock.

The Federal Army of the Potomac under its brave but overconfident commander General Joseph Hooker numbered over 130,000 in five army corps. The more capable General Robert Lee's Confederate Army of

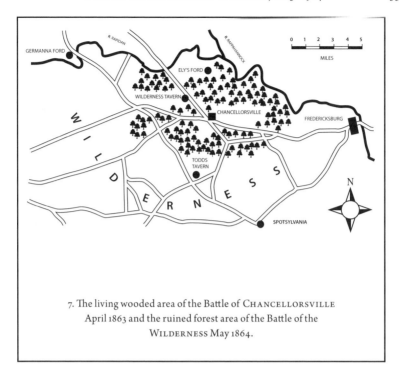

7. The living wooded area of the Battle of CHANCELLORSVILLE
April 1863 and the ruined forest area of the Battle of the
WILDERNESS May 1864.

North Virginia was much smaller, some 60,000. Following his November success, Lee had moved his army into a section of the Wilderness to the west and south of the main western road out from Fredericksburg toward Chancellorsville. This move left Hooker uncertain of the size and dispositions of Lee's army, which remained concealed in the Wilderness and forest in case of an attack from the north.

After the end of the winter lull Hooker planned a wide enveloping movement around Lee's army with the ultimate aim of taking the Confederate capital and ending the war. A part of his force was to be kept near Fredericksburg to contain Lee's army while the main body would move along the lines of the Rappahannock and Rapidan, which they would then cross and enter the forest. There the infantry was first to outflank Lee's left flank and rear and then sweep on turning southward

Fig. 5.1. Chancellorsville. Generals Lee and Jackson planning Jackson's attack on the right flank of the Army of the Potomac. (Artwork by Adam Hook, published in Carl Smith, *Chancellorsville 1863*, courtesy of Osprey Publishing Ltd.)

following the cavalry through the Wilderness in a drive for Richmond. Lee was to be left unable to reply, surrounded on three sides.

At first all seemed to go well. In two days, 29 and 30 April, Hooker's army had reached Chancellorsville in the middle of the forest area and leading elements had marched firmly on through the worst Wilderness into more open Wilderness on Lee's left flank. Lee was equal to the challenge, however. Leading a part of his force to contain the threatening Federal units on the Fredericksburg road, he rushed his main body into the forest clashing with Hooker's infantry front near Chancellorsville. Hooker, almost certainly overestimating the size of Lee's army, ordered a withdrawal and, in so doing, threw away his excellent chance of a victory. Lee and his fellow commander, Thomas "Stonewall" Jackson, seized the opportunity for a crushing response based on sound combat and topographical intelligence. Cavalry patrols located Hooker's right flank regiments in the west side of the forest, and a local resident provided detailed and vitally important information on the narrow tracks through the trees and brushwood, tracks that had been used to transport wood. Use of these tracks enabled Lee to commit Jackson's Corps, some twenty-eight thousand men, to move virtually unnoticed across Hooker's front and mount a surprise attack on the Federal right flank. With Lee's remaining fourteen thousand containing Hooker's force at Chancellorsville, Jackson's men, on 2 May, mounted a ferocious early evening assault, despite first colliding with deer pouring out of the trees on the Federal right flank corps, creating panic and causing Hooker's force to flee across the Rapidan. But in the gathering dusk Jackson was mortally wounded by "friendly fire," and he died a week later.

On the following day, 3 May, Lee's forces attacked from both directions. The forest became filled with smoke, increased by Confederate artillery from guns, including some captured, shooting down from a clearing on a low hill. Hooker withdrew northward to a compact defensive position in the forest near the river. An attack by the Federals on Lee's guard units on the Fredericksburg road was held in check with some difficulty, and Hooker was left with no option but to retreat back across the Rappahannock to his starting line. The fighting had been very costly for both armies. Lee suffered more than 13,000 casualties and Hooker at least 17,500, which, although greater in number, were easier to replace.

The battle that followed a year later, between 4 and 6 May 1864, was fought over a larger area of the Wilderness.[3] The Army of the Potomac, now under Generals Ulysses Grant and George Meade, was slightly smaller than it had been at Chancellorsville with some 110,000 men, 270 guns, and over 600 wagons. It was, however, better led and much more efficient. Grant had had an introduction to fighting in woods at Shiloh in Tennessee in 1862. An initial three infantry corps, to be joined later by a fourth, and a cavalry corps were to cross the Rapidan and attack the right flank of Lee's army in the Wilderness some distance west of Chancellorsville. Grant and Meade were confident that this attack, being simultaneously launched with other army attacks on Richmond from the east and south, would end the war. The North Virginian Army had spent a hard and uncomfortable winter, but morale remained high.

Grant's crossing of the Rapidan and his attack opened a ferocious and bitter two-day battle in the Wilderness; in successive engagements, each side attempted to outflank or split the other army's forces. Soldiers of both armies fought with great determination. Neither side could claim a clear victory, but the battle put a nail in the coffin of the Confederate cause, as the Army of the Potomac marched on to Richmond without incident. The Federals' casualties numbered 2,246 dead, 12,037 wounded, and 3,383 missing, the Confederates' at least 7,500 dead and wounded.[4]

The terrain, harsh enough in the Wilderness woods and thickets, was crossed in several places by muddy ravines. More serious, however, was the general Wilderness surface at springtime, with carpets of dead ivy leaves and fallen twigs which, on many occasions, were set ablaze by musket fire. In one clash, half of a Federal army corps was brought to a halt by forest fires on its front. The fires, which could spread rapidly, particularly took its toll on the wounded lying in the thickets or gathered around the campfires; they were either choked to death or burned alive. Some corpses hung down from tree branches. Whole areas of the battlefield were poorly lit because of the lingering smoke of muskets and were pervaded by the noxious odor of gunpowder, burning flesh, and smoldering wood. Added to the noise of the muskets, at times peaking to as many as ten thousand, and the crashing of trees and branches were often the screams of men trapped by fire, cries lasting through the night. Orders were given by bugle, and the soldiers of both armies shouted when attacking. Because of the limited light and visibility, there were a number of casualties by friendly fire. No campfires were permitted for warming food during the night. Soldiers smoked pipes and exchanged stories of their experiences.

Reconnaissance of opponents' positions was generally based on the reports of patrolling horsemen or skirmishers, and sometimes a lone brave officer would creep boldly from tree to tree to make his own observations. Visibility was sometimes limited to only a few feet ahead, and so the smoke or talk around campfires could even provide better intelligence. A serious difficulty for both armies was the shortage of compasses, and even when they were available, junior leaders were unable to use them and would lose all sense of direction. A favorite tactic was to line men up along the edge of a wood, ready to open fire on opponents entering any clearing before them.

Preceded by skirmishers, attackers would start an advance in lines two or four deep, following orders and, when on the move, acting on bugle commands in the densest parts of the Wilderness. In some areas the thickets were so dense that the advance had to march in single file led by just one soldier crashing backward through the undergrowth and saplings. The numerous separate engagements that characterized the Wilderness Battle were won or lost by the ability of one line's fire to withstand the concentrated fire of the adversary's line in front.

Defense positions were hurriedly built in two or three earthwork strong points protected by fallen timber logs. On the second day of the battle, one corps of the Potomac Army had just sufficient time to construct an abatti. This was assembled some seventy yards in front of the Confederates' forward earthenware bastion, causing attackers to negotiate it and thus providing a target for the defenders' muskets. Soldiers of both armies used trees and stumps as cover.

In the conditions of the Wilderness, flat trajectory artillery was never able to play its full part, as its use was limited to occasions when, in a clearing or on a hillock, gunners could see their opponents or at least see the section of wood or thickets where they believed the opponents to be. Of special effect, however, but only at short range, were canister artillery projectiles, tin cans filled with metal balls tightly packed with sawdust that were lethal when they exploded. Many cavalry units were used for reconnaissance patrols or fought dismounted using their carbines or revolvers, or, if necessary, their muskets. In one action on the second day, a Confederate right wing cavalry brigade charged out of a wood into a clearing to meet a left flanking Federal cavalry brigade commanded by the redoubtable and legendary George Custer. The two brigades met and crossed sabers in the middle, the Federal's band playing "Yankee

Doodle." Custer ordered his right subdivision to make a flank attack through the woods, but this attack was itself outflanked by Confederates and only rescued from disaster by the arrival of a fresh Federal brigade.

The Wilderness battle holds a special place in any record of fighting in woods, forests, and plantations. Other battles produced an equivalent determination to overcome the practical difficulties and fears inspired by forest fighting; such brave determination marked both the Federal and Confederate armies. The huge forest blazes in the Wilderness, however, that burned both fit and wounded soldiers alive, added a grim dimension to the history of forest warfare.

Guerrilla and partisan operations in the war were frequently based in a wood or forest, some from sizable encampments deep within them. The Confederate guerrilla authority was greater than the Federal operation, as it was against Federals in Confederate states or in Federal regions supported by Confederate well-wishers.. Confederate guerrillas went from very small groups armed with sporting weapons or captured muskets, to semi-regular parties supported by Lee, to uniformed mounted units that would make clamorous charges firing their revolvers and raising dust to create the impression of a larger force. New technology had created new targets for guerrillas, particularly railway lines and telegraph wires which were impossible to guard along their entire lengths. Wires would be cut to block communication or to intercept messages or send false ones. Troop movements were often hindered and delayed; not the least of Hooker's problems at Chancellorsville had been attacks by perhaps the ablest of the war's guerrilla leaders, Colonel John Mosby, whose men came to dominate large areas of Virginia. Captured guerrillas were executed by both sides, and occasionally severe communal punishments were exacted.

THE AUSTRO-PRUSSIAN AND FRANCO-PRUSSIAN WARS

In the two wars that followed, those between Prussia and Austria in 1866 and Prussia leading a confederation of north German states against France in 1870–71, only some of the major battles were fought in woods. In the Austro-Prussian conflict, the one major battle between the two massive armies took place at Sadowa (in the present-day Czech

Republic) on 3 July 1866.[5] The Austrians fielded an army of 271,000, under the command of Field Marshal Ludwig Benedek and including a Saxon army under the Saxon Crown Prince Albert. Their opponent's army, under Field Marshal Helmuth Moltke, totaled 278,000. Moltke believed in momentum, moving from mobilization immediately to forward movement. This led him to the strategy of concentrating his three separate armies for a combined entry into Bohemia where they would link up on the line of the Bistritz River: the Elbe Army under General Herwarth von Bittenfeld would be on the right flank, the Second Prussian Army under Crown Prince Frederick William on the left, and the First Prussian Army under Prince Frederick Charles in the center. The Prussian forces were all equipped with the "needle" bolt loading rifle, which was superior to Austrian muzzle loaders. Benedek planned a traditional defensive engagement, relying on his artillery in the center sited on ridges of high ground. Moltke's attack plan aimed at developing actions on both flanks as well as in the center, leading to an encirclement.

At the boundary of the First and Second Prussian Armies and immediately across the river lay two woods: the Swiepwald, some two thousand yards long and one thousand yards wide of densely planted oaks and firs, and, just to the south, the less mature Holawald. Both were in the line of advance of the two army divisions, and both were dominated by the amassed Austrian artillery on the Lipa and Cholm ridges.

The first of these to be attacked by the Prussians was the Holawald lying near the village of Sadowa, some sixteen hundred square yards in size and held by an Austrian Jäger and a Transylvanian Romanian regiment, with an improvised abatti of tree branches at the edge. After taking Sadowa, two Prussian regiments tried to take the wood but sustained very heavy casualties from splinters from the wood's young trees together with ear-shattering shrapnel shells. On one occasion the King of Prussia, Frederick William IV, himself had to urge survivors back into the wood to continue fighting. Survivors recalled that the bombardment and fighting in the wood resulted not only in fatalities but also induced apathy.[6] The Holawald fighting then merged with the adjoining, more difficult fighting in the Swiepwald, which was held by one Hungarian, two Venetian, and one Styrian Jäger battalions and covered by artillery fire from adjacent heights. The Prussians fielded seven battalions and in a spirited attack initially cleared the wood, although officers could only hold their lines of men together with great difficulty under heavy artillery bombardment and with branches and splinters falling upon them. The Austrian Jäger's experience in the use of trees as cover added to the Prussian casualties. The Austrians then tried to retake the wood, one brigade followed by a second, men advancing in a line to the sounds of drums beating and horses neighing, but a powerful Prussian flank attack led to a massacre of the Romanians, Hungarians, and Austrians of the two brigades. The wood continued to draw in additional fresh troops from both sides, and in another fourteen-battalion attack, a Polish regiment was conspicuous for its dash, inflicting heavy casualties on the Prussians in the wood. The dead or wounded from the Prussian First Army in the center now totaled some five thousand from six divisions, and the right-flank operations of the Elbe Army had made little progress. But the timely arrival of the Second Army on the Austrians' exposed right flank, taking Benedek by surprise, reversed the battle immediately to Moltke's advantage. After much heroic fighting the Austrians were forced back across the Elbe in general disorder and, shortly thereafter, accepted defeat.

The Franco-Prussian War of 1870–71 had neither the lengthy forest battles of the American Civil War nor a decisive battle involving woods such as that of the Austrian battle at Sadowa. There were, however, three big battles and many lesser ones throughout the war in which fighting in woods figured, as well as partisan harassment actions later in the war by *francs-tireurs,* several of them launched from woods. The war was decided by the superiority of the Prussian commanders headed by Moltke over the inept and ill-prepared French Army and its leadership. The superiority of the French modern *chassepot* rifle over the Prussian needle gun was not sufficiently great to bring anything more than local successes. Although the *chassepot* was especially useful in woods,. Prussia had a decisive artillery advantage.

The first major action was in the Vosges, where on 6 August 1870 General Charles Froissard's French Army's II Corps fought a battle against superior Prussian and other German formations under the overall command of General Carl von Steinmetz on the heights and foothills of the Spicheren Ridge, three miles south of Saarbrücken. Immediately in front of the ridge were two woods, the Stiftswald and the Gifertswald. Initial attacks by the Prussian First Army, using tree cover for preparation, briefly reached the summit of the ridge, but they were repulsed by vigorous French counterattacks throwing units into confusion and panic. The timely arrival of reinforcements from the Prussian Second Army enabled the Prussians to return the attack from a flank and take an outwork hill feature, the Rotherberg, but a French counterattack mauled the Prussian right wing. A final attack by the Prussians straight up the slopes of the ridge through the trees was threatened by a French flank attack mounted from the Gifertswald, but the Prussians reached the crest as evening darkness closed in. The French, now vastly outnumbered, nevertheless hurriedly improvised a counterattack but this was beaten off by the fire power of the Prussian artillery. The French, their men, and, most important, the last of their reserves, were exhausted by now and withdrew.

The battle was inconclusive, each side suffering casualties of more than four thousand men—either dead, wounded, or missing—but it put an end to the French plans for an invasion of German territory. One detail of the battle merits mention: an attempt by the Prussians to follow up their taking of the Rotherberg after the French retreat by a cavalry pursuit. The Hussar regiment's squadrons met crushing French artillery fire in a narrow forest path. The resulting confusion provided another example of the risks that attend upon the use of cavalry in forests.

At the same time, further east, an even more violent encounter was taking place near the small town of Wörth through which a small river, the Sauer, ran north to south. On the western bank were a series of ridges, most of them covered with trees. Prussian and Bavarian forces totaling seventy-seven thousand with 342 guns under the overall command of the Prussian Crown Prince were deployed on the eastern side of the river. On the northern and western sides, positioned in and around the Froeschwiller and Niederwald woods, were forty-eight thousand French with 167 guns and a few batteries armed with very early machine guns, all under the command of Marshal Patrice MacMahon. The northern Froeschwilles wood included some areas with more brushwood or that were partly cultivated, and the southern Niederwald was composed of

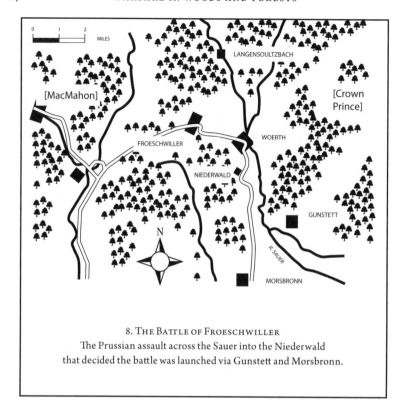

8. THE BATTLE OF FROESCHWILLER
The Prussian assault across the Sauer into the Niederwald
that decided the battle was launched via Gunstett and Morsbronn.

pines well spaced apart—thus permitting infantry and cavalry movement—but also fields of fire for defenders.

MacMahon was long able to hold the Bavarians in the northern
Froeschwiller area, as the Bavarians had become confused and units
lost cohesion in the woods around Langensoultzbach The French, however, were under severe pressure from the Prussians in the center and
south of Wörth. The battle was decided by a Prussian crossing of the
Sauer and their launching of a formidable attack on the French right
flank positioned on the southern Niederwald. The Germans used their
numerical superiority to maximum advantage, which the French were
unable to contain.

In the woodland fighting, the French, in desperation, launched two
cavalry brigade charges, one in the center and the other on their collaps-
ing right flank. The squadrons had to jump over ditches and ride through

hop gardens and tree stumps before even entering the conifer forest. The Germans were well concealed among the trees and in ditches within the forests. They were able to open a murderous fire into the horsemen squadrons as the latter struggled with the terrain; few men from the brigades survived. The Germans were also able to use their massive artillery superiority to devastating effect, at times in full forest areas but more frequently in the clearings between densely wooded areas. The French did, however, score on one occasion when German infantry emerged from a wood into an open area to meet French *chassepot* rifles and machine guns enfilading fire from men concealed in an opposite forest edge. Notable among the French infantry were contingents from French Algeria, the Zouaves, by now an elite and largely but not entirely European regiment, and the "Turcos," Algerian indigenous Tirailleurs. The soldiers of both regiments wore blue, embroidered, open jackets and red, baggy, balloon-style *sarouel* trousers fastened at the shins, a uniform designed for the Saharan sands and totally unsuitable in the trees, branches, and undergrowth of northern Europe. The French colonel commanding the Algerians ordered his men to cover the French withdrawal, declaring: "If necessary we die here, not a single step in retreat."[7] The battle casualties were heavy—the French suffered losses of 10,780 killed or wounded and an additional 6,000 captured by the Prussians, and German losses numbered 11,272 killed, wounded, or missing.[8]

Neither of these battles was decisive, nor did either result in a clear victor. The third, the Battle of Gravelotte on 18 August, provided the French with a costly battlefield success and a strategic defeat.

The Battle of Gravelotte was preceded by a more open engagement at Mars la Tour on the 16th, and was fought as part of the French Army's attempt to prevent the investment of Metz. The French forces, under Marshal Achille Bazaine, numbered 113,000 with 500 guns; the Germans, commanded by Moltke, numbered 187,000 with 732 guns. The French faced west, confronting a German eastward advance toward Metz, their center and left in farm and hilltop positions overlooking a steeply sloping ravine, the Maunce, with their right flank more exposed. German attacks on the French left and center were held, but the German massive artillery superiority enabled the Saxon and the Prussian Guard to turn the right flank and force the French to withdraw.

Fig. 5.2. The Battle of Froeschwiller. Algerian Tirailleurs attacking in the Niederwald.
(Details from a drawing by Edouard Detaille)

The Germans attacking the center and French left found the very thickly wooded slope of the Maunce Ravine unmanageable. The initial attacks were, with one exception, all repulsed. The Germans, underestimating the strength of the French left, ordered a massive attack upon it with disastrous results. The French artillery was able to fire down into the ravine where the utmost confusion prevailed, units falling back upon one another and becoming jumbled together in total disarray on the narrow ravine road with artillery shells bursting in and among the trees. The Germans began a retreat which quickly turned into panic, shrieking soldiers shouting, "We are lost," pouring out of the ravine in flight. Their officers, again including even the Prussian king, attempted to stop the rout with the flat of their swords, in vain.

In tactical terms the local German commander, von Steinmetz, had totally failed to appreciate the difficulties of the terrain, as well as the strength of the French owing to faulty intelligence. Bazaine, the French commander, equally inept, failed to pursue the advantage he had won. In terms of casualties—the Germans lost 20,163 against the French loss of 12,273—appeared at first to be a French success. But the collapse of the right wing and its subsequent withdrawal cut off any relief of Bazaine's army by MacMahon and the later investment of Bazaine at Metz.

There were to be many other smaller-scale forest and woods battles in the war, particularly in the operations of the Army of the Loire in the autumn and winter fighting around the Forêt d' Orléans. Nevertheless, even if not always victorious, the Prussian military training and command structure showed its superiority; the headquarters staff displayed greater flexibility and much better professional judgment than did the badly prepared French Army. This was reflected in the more intelligent command at unit levels, local command and control being as important, if not more so, in woods and forests as in more open country.

The presence of German troops in France led to guerrilla warfare, on a small scale at the outset but turning into more serious raids in the later stages. Some of the *francs-tireurs,* as they were called, were semi-regulars receiving payment; others were entirely irregular. Some men had trained in an amateurish way before the outbreak of the war, and they shot at German columns on the march through Vosges villages and woods; those whom the Germans caught were hung. These guerrillas came from all levels of society; there were aristocrats, members of the bourgeoisie, peasants, urban workmen, and, among them, also a number of foreigners including Poles and Spaniards. They were joined by members of the *Garde Nationale,* firemen, gamekeepers, and forest staff, and later by prisoners of war who had escaped and by men who had fled German-occupied areas. They remained ill-disciplined despite successive government measures to try to control them. They were at their most effective in the wooded areas of north Champagne and also in the Vosges, where from forests they could attack important roads and railway lines, occasionally going over the border into Germany.[9]

THEORETICAL WRITING: LATE NINETEENTH CENTURY

The wars of the nineteenth century, particularly the American Civil War and the Franco-Prussian War of 1870–71, inspired some subsequent detailed and perceptive theoretical analyses. The first of these was the

work of an instructor at the British Army Staff College, Lieutenant-
Colonel H. Schaw, published in 1875.[10] After an initial survey of the different types of wood, density, and undergrowth and their likely effects
on the movement of artillery, cavalry, and infantry, Schaw offered more
practical detail for both attackers and defenders. Trees stop artillery
projectiles, which he claimed were therefore only of value in a bombardment of the edges of a forest, but if the trees form only a small screening
copse, then musket fire remained effective. More doubtfully, he pro-
ceeded to argue that when an attacker had an equal number of men in a
wood as the defender, then the latter had lost the advantage, especially
if the attacker had gained the outer edge, of which the edge nearest the
enemy's main line was vital. Turning to defense, Schaw suggested that
when a wood was too large or too far forward to be held by the defending
army, it could still be denied to an advancing attacker by initially felling
trees and, a little way in, entangling the edge nearest the attacker or even
halfway through the wood if the attacker was to be allowed some entry.[11]
The tree entanglement, if possible, should be in a hollow, a stream, or
a valley line, so that the defenders would have the advantage of height
and a clear view of the assailant; if no valley is at hand, a breastwork
would have to be made with the entanglement belt ideally four rows of
trees from fifteen to twenty yards wide and kept low. The entanglement
should take the form of an abatti, the old idea of fallen trunks or big
branches with boughs cut to form spikes pointing upward in a system
now linked to some standing trees and undergrowth. Defenders would
also be able to fire on the attackers from a sheltered trench, if necessary, protected by a log parapet. This system, Schaw correctly claimed,
had proved a great success in forest encounters in the American Civil
War, protecting the defenders' reserves but at the same time permitting
oblique artillery fire from outside the wood with, he added somewhat
optimistically, only occasional casualties from splinters of wood.

    Such a defense position, a wood with a clearly defined edge and
open ground before it, remained a major defense asset, he claimed,
and still more so if fortified and prepared, including, when necessary,
fortifying salients of the wood and defending any reentrants into the
wood by fire shelter trenches on the flanks. If needed, there could also
be a second line of defense if the terrain so permitted, and, if no paths

existed, lines of communication could be marked by the blazing of trees. To preserve cohesion, Schaw offered defenders the idea of dividing the wood into sections by felling belts of trees, so that defenders knew the sector boundaries and attackers would have difficulty extending any local success. Regarding roads, a passive defense could be achieved by creating roadblocks of fallen trees with their fronts covered by interlocking fire; in a proactive defense, the road would be left open and blocks would be placed only at the wood's edge. Copses or small woods should generally leave their rear open, either for reinforcement or withdrawal. Schaw considered, though later events were to prove him wrong, that well-grown treetops would protect front-line troops and reserves on the ground, and that the real importance of artillery lay at the edges of a wood, repelling an initial attack and firing on any follow-up troops seeking to maintain a momentum.

Schaw concluded by citing four instructive examples from the Franco-Prussian War. The first was the very successful defense by the French of the fortified wood and ravine on the Gravelotte battlefield against a daylong attack by strong German infantry and artillery. Second was the defense of the Bois de Failly and other woods on the Ars-Laquenexy, Mercy le Haut, and Pettre line during the investment of Metz. Next came the defense of woods by cutting belts through them which took place in the woods between St. Cloud and Bougival during the 1871 investment of Paris. Finally, Schaw pointed to the defense of a wood at Woippy near Metz, which had been felled, entangled, and protected from German flanking fire.

A second analysis, also extremely detailed but with broader views over the whole century, appeared in 1892. This, the work of Colonels Robert Home and Sisson C. Pratt, seems to have had an official status as it was published by the British government.[12]

In a general observation on the Franco-Prussian War, the authors note the overall superior performance of the German infantry over the French and its more successful use of woods, citing, in particular, the fighting at Spicheren, Wörth, and the wooded slopes at Mars la Tour and Gravelotte. They judged this superiority to be partly the result of Prussian training which, for drafted soldiers, extended over two and a half to three years full-time and later reserve service. They contrasted, on the one hand, individual training by the Prussians, in which soldiers' self-confidence was developed by encouraging them to think through the capabilities of their body and mind and training them to fight in forests in small groups, with the rigid training of the French, on the other, which discouraged initiative and taught soldiers to fight in large groups and in an extended line followed by a second wave also in an extended line. The Germans trained their junior commanders well, whereas French officers soon lost control in woods. The authors cited, as examples, the chaos in the wood fighting at Sadowa and at the Bois des Genivaux in 1870, when retreating and confused soldiers from different regiments found themselves all mixed up at the rear.

Home and Pratt endorsed Schaw's views on the division of forest areas into sectors with formation, unit, or subunit responsibility for defense and the blazing of trees for the indication of routes. More than Schaw, however, they emphasized the importance of the forward edges of forests in holding a firm defense, with the defenders fully briefed on the support available further within the forest and their lines of withdrawal if necessary. They also took further the concept of lines of abattis; these they urged should be some four hundred to five hundred yards apart with interlocking fire plans. Local conditions would determine the amount of ground to be cleared in front of an edge of forest abatti, the ideal being between fifty and a hundred yards. Specific advice on the felling of trees followed, in some circumstances requiring the trees to be laid with heads pointing toward an advancing opponent and others to be laid parallel to the front, and in all situations a few of the largest trees to be retained as cover for two or three marksmen. Abattis, as well as second lines of defense, had to have secure lines for withdrawal.

The authors continued with arguments concerning artillery, warning that if artillery was to form a main component of the defense of a wood, then guns should be placed some distance away from and on either side of any road leading into the forest, as the road itself would certainly be noted by the attacker as a prime target for his guns. If the guns had to be moved, known tracks or roads should be avoided wherever possible for the same reason and pre-prepared lines of retreat planned. In respect to cavalry, the authors noted the particular value of small woods for the concealment of cavalry planning a flank attack.

More generally, the two colonels drew attention to the importance, as much in forest warfare as anywhere else, of quickly available reserves, both for attacking or defending formations or units. Wherever possible an attacker should make a careful reconnaissance of any wood that he planned to attack; feints could sometimes lead an enemy to give away the sites of his abattis or other defense tactics. Attackers should plan for more than a single attack on a forest, as two or three simultaneous attacks can create confusion among the defenders. Regimental unit and subunit commanders must lead from the front to preserve control and cohesion. Finally, as if looking forward to the eastern front campaigns of the two world wars, the authors accepted that on vast frontages a defending army could build up or hold a continuous line, but maintaining a force at the rear edge of a forest in these circumstances could provide a defender with the opportunity for a surprise attack on any attacker sweeping by.

Both these works, however, convey the impression of somewhat leisurely forest warfare, with sufficient time to prepare a defense or make a sound plan for an attack. The experience of war that followed was, of course, to be more dramatic.

The First World War
1914–17

ALTHOUGH SOME OF THE THEORY advanced by Schaw and Home at the end of the nineteenth century was to prove of value in close combat in the First World War, much was quickly overtaken by the advance in technology, particularly in artillery and machine guns, and the sheer vast scale and prolonged intensity of the war. No army had foreseen the likely nature of land warfare; none had even trained for trenches, let alone forests. Throughout the war numerous battles took place in woods and forests, some large conflicts involving two or more divisions, others involving one or two units but just as hard fought and often as significant politically and militarily as the greater ones. This work can only offer a selection of the most instructive.

The land war can be seen as falling into three main phases. The first consisted of movement on the Western Front as the Germans strove hard to repeat their victory of 1870–71; this phase, which lasted until late September 1914, also included movement on the Eastern Front with the German invasion of East Prussia and the fighting in Galicia that went on longer. The second phase, on the Western Front, was marked by trench warfare battles conducted from long lines of timber-strengthened trenches stretching from the Swiss frontier to the sea. In these battles, fighting for or in a wood, occasionally a forest, was frequently dramatic and bloody. The third phase, in which the German general Ludendorff's final offensive, 1918 offensives, and the later Allied counteroffensive saw a return to movement, also led to battles that the generals of the Seven Years' War would have understood and appreciated.

WESTERN AND EASTERN FRONTS, 1914

In the first phase of the land war, woods and forests largely played the role of topographical features to be used rather than scenes of actual fighting. Armies maneuvered around them to channel opponents into areas of their choice, as targets, to detach some part of the opponent's army, or simply to sideline them away from their own plans of attack, perhaps to be mounted after making preparations concealed among trees. This style of operation was most evident in East Prussia on the Eastern Front and in the Ardennes in the west; in the east it was continued in northwest Poland and the Pripet areas. In the badly conducted Russian campaign in East Prussia, confusion arose when units or formations ran into one another. Alexander Solzhenitsyn offers an account of one such occurrence at a crossroads in the Grünfliess pine forest near Neidenburg, a description clearly based on evidence obtained from survivors. A collision arose from the arrival of two army corps at right angles at the crossroads at night. The forest crossroads "like a black passageway in hell" became a scene of total chaos with "shouting and cursing, the grabbing of reins and shafts, the wrenching aside of wagon-teams by drivers coming the opposite direction, the vehicles pushed into the ditch, the crunch of breaking branches." Eventually, "after dividing, the two masses of men flowed through the forest groping blindly, stopping now and then."[1]

On the Western Front French *chasseurs*, sweating as they traversed the forest-covered Vosges range in the August heat, proved far superior to the German infantry and were able to make a short-lived entry into Alsace. The British Army Expeditionary Force fought three small-scale but notable encounters, all illustrating the hazards of fighting in woods, during the retreat from Mons and the later move to the Ypres salient. On 1 September four British Guards battalions, forming the rear guard of the 2nd Division, fought a spirited battle in a big wood to the north of the small town of Villers-Cotterets.[2] The density of the wood varied: in some areas the trees so close that daylight was restricted and in others trees further apart. Several broad tracks crisscrossed the wood,

the more important ones running east to west along a ridge. Two leading battalions were positioned at the less densely forested edge of the
woods, tasked with holding the German advance and then withdrawing
through the other two battalions, which had been charged with holding the line of the east-west ridge. The leading battalions withdrew as
planned, but meanwhile the German infantry, armed with machine
guns, had crept up from the more densely forested northwestern area
of the wood to attack the left battalion of the two holding the ridge line.
In danger of encirclement, they were rescued by their comrades of the
second battalion in a resolute attack that threw the Germans into such
confusion that they fired on one another.

Later, on 19 September, the Germans used a thick wood referred
to as Hill 189 near the small village of Montreuil to conceal an artillery
battery shelling the British 5th Division, which was attempting to cross
the Marne.[3] The German battery could only be located by the flash of
its guns at dusk. An infantry battalion began a charge through the wood
but were met by a "hail of bullets" from another wood on their right
flank, which pinned them down for some time.

Lastly a small encounter, which occurred when armies were still
maneuvering for position in the Ypres salient in October, merits mention for its originality.[4] Two British battalions were confronting great
difficulty in clearing the Germans out of the wood. The remnant of a
third battalion that had already suffered heavy casualties was ordered in
to reinforce them. The forward two units were informed that reinforcements were coming and were instructed that, when they heard cheering
from behind them in the wood, they were to give the Germans "the mad
minute of rapid fire" and then, when the reinforcements drew close, to
advance in one line cheering, opening rapid fire, and attacking with
their bayonets. Although the remnant of the third battalion had only
some eighty men, they were concealed by trees. The Germans, who until
then had fought hard, turned to flight, only to be chased, shot down, or
bayoneted.

Woods and forests, as they had done over the centuries, continued to provide a refuge, sometimes more apparent than real, both for
civilians terrified by the ferocious battles raging around them and for
soldiers who had either become detached or had detached themselves

from main bodies. The most striking example, a classic tragedy, was the fate of the Russian Second Army and its commander, General Alexander Samsonov, in East Prussia.[5] Both Samsonov and the First Army commander, Pavl Rennenkampf, were cavalrymen with no experience of fighting in woods and forests. With his army outwitted and almost completely destroyed, Samsonov and his headquarters staff began their own withdrawal. Harassed by German detachments, his personal Cossack escort charged, only to be decimated. Samsonov, several staff officers, and one noncommissioned officer were obliged to abandon their horses and take to a forest. It appears that they had no maps and only one compass which lost its value after dusk, when the pathetic little party's supply of matches ran out. To keep going in the darkness they had to link hands. During a halt near Pirnitz Samsonov shot himself. Thick forests, the Grünfliess in particular, provided short-lived refuge from German artillery and machine guns, as well as an escape route for the fortunate from the ill-trained regiments of Samsonov's shattered army. The respite was but brief, as the Germans turned to patrolling and combing sections of forest.

WOODS, FORESTS, AND TRENCHES

In the long second phase of the war a wide variety of new weapons changed the nature of forest warfare. The most important of these was the machine gun, but others of great significance included mortars of various size, barbed wire, grenades and grenade launchers, mines, light field guns, flares, and booby traps.[6] Outside the woods the increased number and size of artillery guns and howitzers had the power to reduce woods to stumps if used in heavy barrages over several days. More commonly the effect of shells, and later aircraft bombs, was reduced in radius by trees, with wood splinters often having the greater effect on ground troops. Another constraint on weapons in woods was the limiting effect on flare illuminations caused by trees. Also, the technique of rolling or lobbing hand grenades along the ground toward the enemy was more difficult in brushwood undergrowth; tree roots could even bounce them back to the sender. Machine guns assisted a forest or wood defender only if the guns had been carefully positioned in advance, in depth, and well concealed to provide maximum surprise. Defenders, too, could usually bring reinforcements forward and evacuate casualties much more rapidly. A soldier captured by a defender usually had a much better chance of ending up in a prisoner-of-war camp than a soldier taken by an attacker who had no men to spare for guard or escort and instead would opt for a final solution.

The dense nature of forests and woods made traditional fire and movement tactics difficult, if not impossible, for attackers. Instead, platoon lines of riflemen and grenade throwers two deep and six feet apart would move forward with a second platoon immediately behind supported by a machine-gun team or section. A similar grouping from a second battalion would follow thirty to fifty yards behind for support or consolidation, thus bringing it to a four- and possibly six-wave attack. In 1915 the attackers were still at a disadvantage, as the machine-gun section had to be positioned before they could open fire. Whether the men of the second platoon or the second following battalion should leapfrog through the leading waves of attackers or halt to avoid a "traffic jam" was much debated and, in any case, depended on each individual situation. It was generally hoped that machine-gun sections might work their way around to a flank, often feasible in open country but much more difficult in a forest.

Machine guns positioned on the edges of forests could, however, give defenders a greater advantage against attackers trying to cross open ground before the forest edge; one problem was that some woods degraded into brushwood or scrub at their edges. Later in the war attackers could obtain protection against gunfire from a forest edge by covering the gunfire from armored cars or tanks, provided they could spot flashes of fire and know exactly where the defenders were. Finally, at the other end of the weaponry scale, the bayonet now played its grim role in all close-quarter forest fighting. The importance of training for the most effective use of these weapons and tactics was clear, but the need for manpower at the front was too often considered the priority. As we shall see, regiments, particularly those recruited hurriedly and trained even more hurriedly, lacked the skills and leadership experience necessary for warfare in general but particularly for fighting in forests.

The soldier's traditional fear of the "unknown," what may lurk deep inside a forest, hitherto a big advantage for any defender, had by 1916 become modified by the prolonged artillery bombardments that came to precede attacks. These bombardments, reducing forests to stumps stripped of branches, could sometimes show an attacker the presence or movement of defenders, especially if trained watchers, balloons, or aircraft were available. Generally, if trench lines could be dug amid tree roots, which was not always feasible, they would be dug a little distance from the edges but still giving the defenders a clear view over intervening ground. On some occasions trench lines were dug right through a wood. Mines and booby traps placed in woods served defenders well. Gas bombardments could pave the way for a successful attack or strike an opponent's troops known to be in a wood preparing a defense. Many photographs, official and private, portray the devastation in woods that had been the scene of severe fighting.

THE SOMME BATTLES: VERDUN

Some of the sharpest battles in and around woods and forests in this second phase of the war were in the British section on the Western Front, the Somme from July 1916 onward and, for the French, the long drawn-out battle around Verdun beginning in February. Although the Germans were aware that a major British offensive was impending, the great trees of Aveluy Wood had concealed much of the camp's accumulation of ammunition and stores needed for the offensive. The battles that followed the very bloody opening day, on 1 July, lay on the roads to the small town of Bapaume, with fierce fighting in several woods between July and October. Later, in 1917, equally violent fighting took place farther north at Bourlon Wood. In the long French sector, perhaps the bloodiest fighting of the whole war was at Verdun following the first German offensive in February 1916 through to October. Small woods were reduced to a lunar landscape.

In the British Somme area, the Germans used large and small woods and copses for ambushes and assaults as the British struggled to make progress around Thiepval and on the roads to Bapaume. Each encounter,

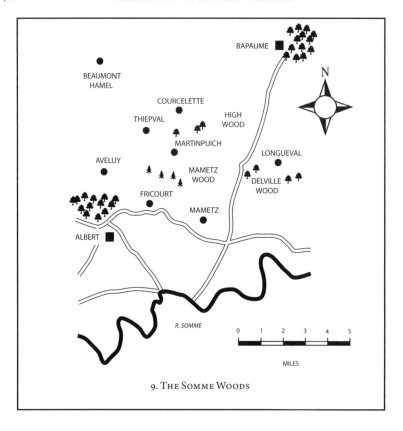

9. THE SOMME WOODS

even in small woods and copses, cost lives, and the larger ones hundreds. The first of the major Somme woods battles was that of Mametz Wood, some 220 acres in size, one mile stretching north and south but two hundred to three hundred yards wide lying across the line of advance.[7] Described as a "menacing wall of gloom," the forest had been untended for two years and the undergrowth was almost impossible to walk through. The trees were huge oaks some nine feet in girth and beeches of two feet, the average height between thirty-five and forty-five feet. Inside the wood was a central ride running north to south and two running east to west. It was defended by a Prussian Guards Reserve division. The Germans had prepared wire and machine-gun posts along the forest's edges and trench lines linked to lines in the wood itself. The task of taking the wood was given to the New (Kitchener) Army Welsh 38th Division; it had had sound open-country training but, amazingly, nothing at all relating to forests. The 17th Division was to attack the southern and western edge of the wood at the same time as the main 38th Division attacked from the east. Together the two divisions were greatly superior in number.

The 17th Division assault, illuminated by flares, opened at 2 AM on the morning of 7 July, with poorly coordinated artillery and smoke barrage; the assault by the 38th Division followed later. Both attacks suffered heavy casualties from machine guns and mortar fire in the open ground before the forest edge, the artillery bombardment having had only limited success, and no lasting advance was made. Both division commanders were removed. The next attack, in successive waves, one hundred yards apart with four paces between each man, followed on the 10th after an artillery bombardment, but the leading waves soon broke in the face of heavy German machine-gun fire, the difficulties of the dense undergrowth, and overhead bursts from the division's own artillery, again poorly coordinated. The Welshmen made slow progress, occupying much but not all of the forest by day's end. The conditions struck horror: parties of men had lost their way and their unit, barricades had formed from fallen tree branches on which were lying whole or dismembered dead, the corpses of snipers were hanging from trees, most of the smaller trees had been reduced to jagged stumps, and shell holes could be seen every few yards. Wounded men tried to climb over tree trunks and branches in search of help. A fresh division, the 21st, was ordered in to replace the decimated and exhausted 38th, and Mametz Wood was only finally cleared on 12 July.

Farther south of Bapaume lay two other important woods, Delville Wood of 160 acres on the eastern side of a local road flanking the town and High Wood, only slightly smaller, to the west. From both, the Germans launched strong enfilading fire not only on the road but also from spurs and salients of both woods on much of the surrounding country. The first attack on High Wood was made on 15 July. It benefited from a Royal Flying Corps reconnaissance aircraft that deliberately flew low over the wood to draw German fire, thus revealing the German positions. These were noted by the pilot and a message dropped to help the attacker.[8] But the attack was a failure, owing as much to leaves and branches from fallen trees obscuring the view, saplings, brambles,

Fig. 6.1. German Observation Post, Trones Wood, Somme.
(Courtesy of the Imperial War Museum, photo no. Q 862)

thorns, and creepers, as to well-positioned German snipers. Another
attack on the 20th also failed. The wood was only taken later on 15 September, at great cost, by the 47th (London) Division. Because New
Zealanders along the road were near the western edge of the wood, the
Londoners could not be given the artillery support that they needed,
even though a massive mortar support had been laid on.[9] The division's
plan of attack had also provided for the support of four tanks. The sector
Army Corps commander, ignoring advice, insisted that the tanks should
support the infantry going through the wood, but the tree stumps prevented this and the tanks achieved nothing. The German defense was
tenacious, soldiers using shell craters in the absence of a trench system
and later mounting vigorous but unsuccessful counterattacks. After the
wood was captured, one sergeant remarked:

> We had been ordered to defend High Wood to the last, real eerie it was
> I can tell you, we were fighting our rearguard action on ground that was
> weed infected with shell craters, brambles covering the tree stumps and
> fallen trees, there were decaying trenches, decaying skeletons and rusty
> wire entanglement everywhere.[10]

The division suffered over forty-five hundred casualties. Earlier fighting had cost even greater numbers.

The first attack on Delville Wood was mounted at the same time as that on High Wood, 15 July, but this wood, with its thick undergrowth, was not cleared until mid-September. This first attack was preceded by an artillery bombardment of more than 350 guns which, despite wet weather, set the wood on fire. The attacking 9th Division, composed of one brigade each of Highland and Lowland Scots and one brigade of South Africans, captured much of the wood in a two-stage attack, but only in the face of strong German counterattacks and artillery fire. The last assault, to clear a salient on the southeast corner, began in August and continued into September. An assault planned for 3 September met with heavy German opposition. It began in the early evening when light was already failing. The attackers were confronted by thick barbed-wire barricades, with fallen tree trunks making visibility very poor. The ground was a mass of broken wire, fallen trees, and hastily dug trenches, a nightmare scene, the glare from bursting shells only serving to show more clearly the gaunt devastation. The support of three tanks, their first appearance on a battlefield, had been promised for the final assault on the 15th. Only one actually arrived, but the terrain within the wood, a carpet of tree stumps, again proved too difficult for the tank to proceed.[11] Fighting became very close-quarter, only a few yards separating men armed with rifles, bayonets, and grenades, but eventually the last German was cleared from the woods.[12]

One feature of both the High Wood and Delville Wood operations was poor staff work. Formation commanders should have asked for, and been given, much more detailed topographical intelligence.[13] The plan for the July High Wood attack had actually included a sweep through the wood by cavalry regiments, one from the Indian Army; this proved a costly failure. In September no one had thought through what the very

early tanks might be able to do in such terrain. No proper training in forest operations had been given to the attackers; extended line advances
were mowed down by concealed machine guns. Aircraft intelligence
and commanders' preference to hold a front line against German counterattacks rather than to defend in depth also had severe consequences.
The grim dehumanizing nature of this wood fighting is summed up in
a divisional history:

> It may be said that in this gruesome position in which were so many
> dead, dying and badly wounded, it was amusing to observe the German
> marksmen falling from the trees, with a heavy thump to the ground. The
> moral effect of this touch of humour which instantly struck all, was amaz-
> ing. The wounded became cheery, the exhausted gained new life.[14]

The huge-scale Verdun battles fought by the French Army in 1916
saw duels to the death in hilly country, which included a number of
woods, each one fought over with a tenacity that has few equals in the
history of war. Many woods came to be reduced to the same wasteland
as the more open areas. Between 21 February and 15 July (and the battles
were to continue until December) German artillery had fired some
twenty-two million shells into the salient, and the French had replied
with some fifteen million.[15] Soldiers fought, attacked, and defended
improvised trenches and shell craters in the remains of the woods. A
postwar guidebook's selection of photographs capture soldiers' lives
and actions in the woods. These include a trench system in the Argonne
woods, infantrymen in a wood throwing bombs from a rough trench, a
runner hurrying on a track through a ruined wood, the ruins of a wood
one mile from Verdun's Fort Douaumont, a gas bombardment of French
positions in a wood whose trees have lost all leaves and most branches,
cooks carrying soup to frontline soldiers in a wood, and trenches and
an observation post in a wood with trees entirely stripped of branches.[16] Another especially striking photograph, also taken in 1916, shows
the Ravin de le Dame, called the "Ravine of Death" by soldiers, near
Douaumont. The scene inspired the novelist Arnold Zweig to write:
"The grey figures of venerable tree roots became entangled with each
other. Laid low into the sun these great trees rot away. Here, man, in the
space of a few months had ravaged the creation of nature over human

generations."[17] French soldiers came to have a particular dread of German flame-throwers with their capability of setting a wood on fire and causing much personal injury. The intensity of the fighting frequently broke up unit cohesion and reduced surviving soldiers to seek refuge in single holes in open ground or on the forest floor—"each in his hole, alone, horribly alone," in the words of Charles de Gaulle.

The battle for Bourlon Wood, the last stage of British Army operations in the Somme area until late 1918, has been overshadowed by the battles collectively known as "Third Ypres" fought mainly in mud. But Bourlon Wood is still of interest as an example of how fighting over a 640-acre wooded hill can influence and play a significant role in a major operation. The wood, formed of closely packed trees with dense undergrowth, gullies, and marsh, was included in the defense line to which the Germans had withdrawn in late 1916 and early 1917, known to the British as the "Hindenburg Line." The aim of the British Third Army tasked with the major operation was to take the town of Cambrai. One sector of the army's front, that opposite Bourlon Wood, was allotted to two divisions. The prime objective of the first, the 47th (London) Division, was to clear the wood and enter Boulon village on the far side of the wood; the second division, the 59th (North Midland), was to provide support on the right flank, the east side of the wood, as well as on the western side.[18] Planned for 20 November 1917, the attack was expected to last for only twenty-four hours, but by the night of the 21st forward troops had only reached the open ground leading up to the hill, having suffered severe casualties from German machine guns in the wood. The next attack was launched at dawn on the 23rd in cold and snowy weather; the troops were tired and had had no training in forest fighting. The two forward brigades were supported by twelve tanks and fifty aircraft firing into the trees. The infantry advance followed a seventy-gun artillery creeping barrage but could make little progress against German strong points in the wood's clearings; further, the tanks experienced great difficulties amid the trees, both standing and fallen, and German fire. By evening German resistance, artillery fire in particular, had brought the advance to a halt on both the center and the flanks. Visibility had been reduced to almost nil, and trees were crashing down. Fresh formations and battalions arrived with orders to continue the attacks on the following days in order to clear the wood and the village, but the Germans maintained a pattern of local counterattacks and the few tanks that had not been put out of action or broken down were forced to withdraw. German artillery fire now included phosgene gas shells as well as high explosives. The planned attacks, which were supposed to have been supported by additional tanks that never arrived, failed, and by the evening of the 25th the British had been forced back from several areas that they had gained. Dead British soldiers in the wood were simply pushed out of the way; only those who could walk were evacuated. Many of the soldiers had lost all sense of direction and did not know in which direction to withdraw. The attacking division had lost more than four thousand men—killed, wounded, or missing.

Despite the casualties, the icy rain, the difficulties of supply and intelligence, and that substantial German reinforcements had arrived, a further attack by the Guards Division regiments was ordered for the 27th. By now, following rain, snow, and shell fire, the floor of much of the wood was ankle deep in mud, adding to the difficulties of both sides in digging even small protective scrapes among the tree roots. At the end of the day, and after heavy casualties, all the battalions in the wood and on the flanks were back at their starting lines. The 28th saw little movement but bore the brunt of a very heavy German high-explosive and gas bombardment of the wood. The gas used was, again, phosgene, now recognized as a sign that an attack will follow, as the gas disperses quickly; in contrast, the more dangerous mustard gas can linger on, its odor remaining in the forest dips, ditches, and other ground cavities for several days after a bombardment. Mustard gas, accordingly, was only used when the army firing its shells was not expecting to move into the area bombarded. The next day, the 29th, the Royal Engineers succeeded in building a double-apron wire barricade in front of the areas of the wood that still remained in British hands.

On the 30th the Germans mounted a large-scale counterattack involving the wider front thirteen divisions, of which five were to strike in the Bourlon area. Within the wood the wire barrier proved its worth, although the defending London Territorials suffered severely from repeated phosgene and high-explosive bombardments.[19] On 2

December the decision was made to withdraw all British divisions to a winter line farther south, a move completed on the 7th.

The local winner of the long battle of Bourlon Wood was the Crown Prince Rupprecht of Bavaria. But one of the strategic aims of the British Commander-in-Chief, Sir Douglas Haig, had been to ease the pressure on the Italian Army which had just suffered a catastrophic defeat at the hands of the Austrians. German reinforcements from Russia, which were planned to follow up on this success and force Italy out of the war, had to be redirected to the Cambrai area which the Germans expected would remain quiet. Thus Bourlon Wood had not been fought entirely in vain.

The First World War
1918

———

THE LAST YEAR OF THE WAR, 1918, saw dramatic change. First, the German Army on the Western Front received massive reinforcements, more than forty divisions, following Russia's withdrawal from the war, enabling it to return to the offensive. Second, the U.S. Army arrived in France in rapidly accelerating numbers, in divisions over twenty-five thousand strong; and third, armies, first the German and later the Allies, developed equipment and tactics to break the trench stalemates and return mobility to the battlefield, most notably aircraft and tanks.

At line regimental levels experience gained was put to good use, to become evident on all terrains including woods and forests. Fully effective re-equipment appeared in all armies. French regiments, which in 1914 had but four machine guns, now had thirty-six. British battalions, which in 1914 had at most four, more commonly two, light machine guns, now had thirty and some mortars. In the German armies each infantry rifle company had, by 1918, six machine guns and each battalion one heavy machine-gun company and six mortars. The large American battalions, over one thousand men strong, went even further. Each of four rifle companies included four platoons structured to include detachments for grenade throwing, rifle grenade discharges, and four light machine guns to support an assault rifle squad. Three battalions made up a regiment which also included three light field guns, six mortars, and a heavy machine-gun company. The French Chauchat light machine gun, which could be fired from the shoulder, and the portable tripod version of the British Lewis light machine gun could both be brought into action quickly for close-quarter fighting. Improved signal systems had brought artillery under better all-arms control. Aircraft had moved on from air dogfights to attacking troops on the ground and among trees with machine guns and bombs. French and British officers had learned lessons, although in both countries manpower problems had reduced the number of divisions in the field. Americans had much yet to learn.

BELLEAU WOOD

Fighting on the Western Front from February to July consisted of efforts, often desperate, to contain the strength and ferocity of powerful German offensives made possible by the increased troop strengths. The last of these offensives was to bring the Germans back again to the Marne in the Chateau-Thierry area, opening operations leading to the Second Battle of the Marne. In this prolonged series of engagements the newly arrived American troops were to play a leading role, most notably General James Harbord's 2nd Division, a formation composed of two brigades, one the U.S. Army and the other the U.S. Marine Corps. Each brigade was formed into two regiments of three battalions each; the division possessed division artillery, machine guns, and mortar support units. Their training had been patchy, officers' tactical training especially weak. The division had gained some earlier combat experience, but this had not included any forest fighting. At the outset it was largely dependent on French artillery and French aircraft support, but the latter was only available infrequently, leaving the air free for German air observation. A weakness that became evident early on was that drafts replacing casualties had only basic and no continuation training; moreover, even when later training improved, subunit cohesion suffered, particularly in conditions when small detachments could easily be split up.

After some initial confusion in the French regional command under which the 2nd Division had been placed, it was ordered to participate in a large counteroffensive involving several French divisions. The American division was tasked to attack on the east flank of the German salient at Chateau-Thierry.[1] The U.S. Army and Marines then set out on a learning curve notable for the gallantry of its soldiers but also for the confusion among its officers. The six Marine Corps battalions of

10. THE MARNE: JULY 1918

the 4th Brigade supported by the brigade's machine-gun battalion were
tasked to lead the attack. In its line of advance lay a dense kidney-shaped
forest, one thousand yards long, called Belleau Wood, held by the German 237th Division, below full strength but including one Major Hans
Bischoff, an officer with experience in wood fighting in Africa, probably
at the battle of Waterberg in South West Africa in 1904 where artillery
and machine guns were used. The wood, one of tall hardwood trees,
was in full summer leaf with heavy undergrowth concealing boulders
and ravines. American forward units reached the area of the wood on 3
and 4 June, to receive a German mortar and artillery barrage. The division's commander and his staff had neither topographical nor combat
intelligence to hand, and they seriously underestimated the German
strength. Poor coordination with the French worsened matters, with
the Marines suffering casualties from French fire. The approach to the

wood on the 5th began with a limited artillery preparation, and Marines advancing through fields suffered severe casualties from German fire from the wood.

Bischoff's plan for the defense of the wood was based on no fewer than two hundred machine guns which he distributed along three lines of defense among the trees and undergrowth—the strongest in the north, one in the narrow center, and the third in the south. Each line had concealed barbed wire and timber protection trenches, and fire plans of machine guns, mortars, and snipers. A further asset for the German defense was observation reports on American movements from balloons and aircraft. The Marines first dawn advance to make contact on the 6th across the remaining fields was in open order, a few feet between the men in an extended line, platoon following platoon, a massacre target for the German machine gunners. A second attack in the afternoon in another sector of the wood met with the same German reception. There had been no artillery support for either of the attacks and no preliminary reconnaissance. In each attack the few men who managed to enter the wood broke up into small, disorganized groups attempting to take on the well-protected German machine-gun positions with grenades and bayonets. Fighting became chaotic, confusion replaced command, and a German bombardment added to the casualties. The bombardments continued into the evening and throughout the night. All that had been achieved by the end of the day was the occupation of one area in the southern portion of the wood, this at a cost of more than one thousand dead or wounded Marines.

The German defense was motivated by an additional factor. The High Command, faced with the arrival in France of an apparently endless stream of U.S. divisions, perceived a need to hit the Americans early and hard to bring them into disrepute and destroy morale and self-respect. For this purpose, two fresh first-class divisions were brought forward, their vanguards entering the wood. American attacks were resumed on 10 June, this time with artillery support but still revealing the Marines' inexperience; some did not even carry their rifles at the ready, and many had not been issued grenades. One unit suffered particularly severely from machine-gun fire from the wood, again while advancing across fields. Arriving in the wood on the 11th amid dim early-morning light, fog, and smoke, this unit's commander ordered an advance to the northeast, but in the confusion he advanced to the southeast. Then, after successfully destroying a German unit, the Marine commander proudly reported that his men had cleared the entire wood. The day ended with the Marines' colonel unsure of his location and the divisional commander ensuring that the American media at home was proclaiming a victory. Recriminations weakening the authority of senior officers followed.

On the 12th the Marines resumed their northward attacks. The artillery's light French 37-mm guns were of little use in the thick forest, and the heavier artillery was fired too far behind the German defense lines in the belief that the Marines held more of the wood than they did. But now attacking in small groups rather than in lines, shouting the Marine battle cry *Eee-ya-yip* and losing men in the face of German machine guns, they eventually managed to claim, in some disorder, the northern side of the wood.

On 19 June the fighting opened with a German counterattack, which was contained, but a further German artillery and gas attack disorganized the U.S. command and regained some ground for the Germans, all at additional heavy cost to both sides. On the American side the 7th Infantry Regiment was brought in from the 3rd Division to relieve the Marines; the infantry's officers believed that the battle was almost over. They made successive attacks from the 16th to the 21st to complete the clearing of the wood, in the process losing more than three hundred casualties, but the task was beyond them. On the 22nd the Marines were brought back, and, despite their earlier casualties, a battalion attack was launched on the next day. Four companies, in an extended line, advanced across barbed wire, undergrowth, and tree stumps into the usual hail of machine-gun fire. Although given strengthened artillery and mortar support, they were only able to gain two hundred yards. More artillery was believed to be the answer, and on the 24th an eighteen-battery barrage lasting fourteen hours was opened on the remaining German positions in or near the wood. A final assault on the 25th initially met with some vigor by the Germans but finally broke their control and command, survivors either surrendering or trying to escape. By the evening Belleau Wood was a Marine Camp. In the three weeks of fighting to take a wood one thousand yards long, the total U.S. Army and Marine Corps casualties numbered 1,811 killed and 7,966 wounded.[2]

The whole battle is instructive in any history of fighting in a dense unknown forest.[3] Inadequate preparation and intelligence, inexperienced command and staff control, overconfidence—all these factors, unfortunate anywhere, were to prove disastrous in a forest fight. Nevertheless, after Belleau Wood, the Germans treated the Americans with respect, and experience gained by the Americans was to prove useful in dealing with the smaller woods of the Argonne in September.

SECOND BATTLE OF THE MARNE

The main Second Battle of the Marne, from 18 July to 7 August, was fought in several wood and forest areas in the wide salient created by the German advance between Reims and Soissons, reaching and briefly crossing the Marne at Chateau-Thierry.

The west flank of the Chateau-Thierry salient was the more threatening, as it was nearer to Paris. To contain the threat on the extreme left was the French Tenth Army commanded by the aggressive General Charles Mangin, appointed to this command at the insistence of the French prime minister, Clemenceau "The Tiger." In one part of his army's front lay the Forest of Villers-Cotterets. Although his troops were shaken, exhausted, and underfed, their ranks reduced by Asian influenza, Mangin wished to counterattack. General Philippe Pétain, the French army commander, denied him the additional formations that he requested for his plan. General Ferdinand Foch, the Allied commander-in-chief, countermanded Pétain's refusal, and the attack, as part of a general front offensive by five French armies together with a British and an American army corps, was prepared for the morning of 18 July.

Faced with low morale, war weariness, and desertions from his army, Mangin decided to depart from the common practice of French generals choosing comfortable chateaux or *mairies* for their headquarters and, instead, to impose his aggressive leadership and demands on his dispirited soldiers more directly. As an observation site, he selected a log cabin on the edge of the Retz Forest mounted high above the foliage of the forest's oaks and beeches, trees fifty feet tall and in full leaf, a cabin originally occupied by forest rangers on the lookout for forest fires. Tents and cabins for field telephones were placed at the base. Despite some mist, Mangin both secured his view and cemented his authority.

Mangin's plan was to use the Villers-Cotterets Forest to conceal the main thrust of his army's attack; in the event, concealment was helped by mist and heavy rain. There was to be no preliminary bombardment, and artillery support would take the form of a creeping barrage in front of an infantry assault at dawn. Frenchmen, together with Algerian and Moroccan Tirailleurs, black African Tirailleurs, and even a regiment of the Foreign Legion, pushed through and out of the wood into open ground. There the Germans were pursued by tanks and aircraft.

In the course of the battle, on the morning of the 18th, Pétain visited Mangin's observation post and remarked, coldly, that it was "fine, perhaps a little too fine." He then said that since the Germans had actually crossed the Marne the Tenth Army should now take up purely defensive positions, upon which he left. Mangin turned to his chief-of-staff, declaring that because Pétain had not given any direct order to stop the attack, he would therefore continue it. He then referred his decision to Foch, who warmly agreed. Mangin's epic determination paid off, producing a forest victory he could justly claim as his own.[4] The Germans, as exhausted as the French, were unable to withstand the desperate French assault, and the French formation marching out of the Villers-Cotterets Forest marked the end of the last German offensive in the war.

Fighting on the eastern side of this front was more difficult, as there were many hills and ridges, and the Forêt de la Montagne de Reims, with smaller woods surrounding it, had been neglected for four years by French forestry staff. It was now choked with high summer undergrowth which, in the words of one historian, "often [made it] hard to force a way [through] even when there was no opposition."[5] In mid-July the most dense, impenetrable sector was being held by French and Italian formations, the latter described as being in an "exhausted and shaken condition." Foch sought immediate help and, in response, Haig sent four British divisions; two of these —the 51st (Highland) and 62nd (West Riding)—were attached to the French Fifth Army on the east, initially only as a reserve but almost immediately were ordered to attack. They arrived in great haste after long journeys with scarce provisions of food

Fig. 7.1. Capture of a German prisoner, Second Battle of the Marne.
(Courtesy of the Imperial War Museum, photo no. Q 11086)

or water and sometimes none at all. The divisions included a number of young soldiers who had recently arrived in France. The commanders and officers had no experience fighting in forest conditions, French maps were neither reliable nor easy to understand, and, prior to the attack, there was no time for ground reconnaissance or a handover with the French. They were, however, aided by air reconnaissance reports and, when targets presented themselves, with air-to-ground bombing and machine gunning.

A four-division attack—including two French and two British divisions—was launched on 20 July to pinch out the German salient, each British division taking up either side of the river Ardre in the steep tree-covered hills of three small villages: Marfaux, Bligny, and Chau-muzy.[6] It was mosquito weather: very hot, with occasional showers. Eight battalions led the attack. In the general haste and confusion, some regiments first had to make an approach march at night through almost pitch-black forests to reach their assembly areas. The woodlands tracks were often under German artillery fire and casualties were sustained. Of the last stage of this approach march, one officer wrote in his diary:

> The tracks hitherto quite respectable now became a mere narrow space between trees, and later on, into a mere nothingness. Thick blackness was everywhere excepting a faint illumination showing where the tops of the trees were. On and on we stumbled in single file colliding with trees and with our neighbours and plunging into deep holes full of sticky mud . . .

> On arriving in the assembly area he found himself and his company in terrain where forest conditions were changing logistics:

> . . . disentangling ourselves from Italians, French, another unit of our division, motor lorries, French transport, ammunition wagons, guns, lim-bers and mules; countless mules—mules carrying rations, mules carrying water, mules carrying ammunition and more (spare) mules.

In the further advance to the starting line the officer's own battalion became "mixed up at some crossroads with a crowd of units from dif-ferent divisions and of seemingly different nationalities." With a French guide for each company, "once more we plunged into the horrors of those forest depths, and in the early morning [into] these dark woods with their muddy paths and their foul stenches of poison gas and decay-ing bodies of horses."[7]

The element of surprise was difficult to achieve; in any case, the two German divisions in the forest were expecting an attack. Battalions lost direction amid the trees and men from different units got mixed up with one another; compass bearings added to the confusion when their mea-suring points were wrongly identified. The preliminary French creeping artillery barrage, moving a hundred meters every four minutes, started one thousand yards ahead of the attacking infantry leaving concealed machine-gun posts in the woods unscathed, to open fire on the attacker from unexpected directions. There had been no time to coordinate a fire plan to concentrate fire locality by locality, or to use gas. Finally, the French guns fired shells with a sensitive high-explosive fuse which would explode in the foliage, not only posing the danger of splinters but also creating unnerving echoes. Ten minutes after the start of the attack, German artillery fire fell on target avenues of attack that their gunners had anticipated. Casualties were heavy, with one battalion losing as many as four hundred men. Because of the hurried move to the area of much of the division's support services, in the early phase many of the wounded had to be taken away in French ambulances and hospital trains. The German units were high quality and fought stubbornly, using their concealed machine guns with skill and frequently counterattacking. One of the attacking battalions changed its tactic from platoon lines to rushes by sections, throwing bombs into dugouts whenever the undergrowth permitted, but this tactic was barely more successful. On the 20th one of the divisions, the 62nd, suffered the loss of 46 officers and 775 soldiers. The 51st Division had succeeded in advancing about a mile into the wood, but the victory was achieved at excessive cost: a few outposts had been taken but the main German lines remained and were reinforced by four more divisions.

The fighting in the dense woods and villages continued until the 28th. Massed German machine guns continued to mow down the lines of advancing Yorkshiremen and Highlanders as they struggled to advance through cornfields to the edges of the forest; the same was repeated among the trees. Only in the last days of the battle did the Germans begin to show any signs of weakness and withdrawal, at which time the fighting could move into more open country, where aircraft and tanks could come into play.

This forest warfare, new for the two British divisions, had proved almost as difficult for their artillery as for their infantry. Their division batteries, which arrived late on the 20th, had to move frequently and had no protection other than what they could dig for themselves. In one attack, on the Marfaux area, some guns fired as many as six hundred rounds each. Communication in the forest was exceedingly difficult and ammunition supply even more so, occasionally being bombed by German aircraft. The machine-gun companies worked together with the artillery, learning how to give support while on continuous advance through the trees. Engineers cut paths, marking them with tapes. A few days into the offensive casualty clearing stations were set up and the two divisions' field ambulance detachments opened up treatment centers among the trees for the more seriously wounded.

The last two days saw the two British divisions, together with one French division, making a slow advance on the 27th. Their creeping artillery barrage through the forest totaled 120,000 rounds fired in salvoes at a pace of one hundred meters every eight minutes with, because of the density of the wood, three twenty-minute pauses. The Germans, however, had already withdrawn.

The French had hoped to use a few light Renault tanks on paths and tracks in the forest but the ground was too sodden. Instead, to guard against a trap, in a fine eighteenth-century touch, a horsed reconnaissance regiment, put together from Australian and New Zealand cavalry and men from a New Zealand cyclist battalion, was sent out on patrol in the forest. A final British and French attack beginning on the 28th, when the ground had become more open, brought the Second Battle of the Marne to an end on 7 August. Later, in September Argonne operations, Americans were able to use the light French Renault tank on pathways through the forests.

The events in the four years of the war showed how woods and forests still remained important impediments for any attack or advance, and how effective a defense trees could provide. Despite this, however, the official British Army assessment of the lessons of land conflict in the war contains no mention of forest or wood combat.[8]

The Second World War

1939–45

WARFARE FROM 1939 TO 1945 WAS dominated by the use and development of late-1930s military technology, particularly with regard to armor and aircraft. Paradoxically, however, the war would also see dramatic use of forests in the Soviet Union's battles with the German Army, and in the war's last months would see the biggest forest battle in recorded history.

THE RUSSO-FINNISH WINTER WAR, 1939–40

The main events of the Second World War were preceded by a conflict only indirectly related to that between Nazi Germany and Britain and France. This so-called "Winter War," which began with the Soviet Union's attack on Finland in November 1939 and lasted until March 1940, was to provide one of the most striking chapters in the history of forest fighting. Finland, a small country, could field an army of only nine under-strength divisions at the outset; these were soon to receive reinforcements from recalled reservists and a territorial civil guard. But the army possessed no tanks of any value, no antiaircraft guns, inadequate and obsolete artillery, and very few antitank weapons. The Finnish infantry, however, did possess a good 7.62-mm rifle and an excellent submachine gun, the kp 31 Suomi. The Soviet invaders totaled twenty-one divisions, each much larger than those of the Finns, all well equipped with tanks and artillery and able to call up massive air support. As the campaign progressed, Soviet reinforcements heightened this imbalance in numbers. Yet the Finnish Army was well trained, well clothed,

11. THE WINTER WAR: 1939–40.

and highly motivated, whereas the 1939 Red Army was overconfident, poorly led and trained, and lacked basic winter clothing as well as any real enthusiasm in some units, despite their massive numbers. The Finnish forces, under the command of Marshal Carl Gustav Mannerheim, were deployed first to defend their pre-prepared line of fortifications and forests and later on the Karelian Isthmus; their second task, aided by their skillful use of winter warfare, namely, ski-equipped fast-moving groups, was to inflict severe punishment on the Red Army in the central and northern sectors of the long border frontier.

The nature of the central and northern frontier territory, much of it thick, snowbound pine forest, forced the Red Army to move along the few existing roads, most of which were narrow. Heavy snow and cold added to the Soviet difficulties. The Finns, despite their numerical inferiority, were able to commit local forces capable of harassing, often immobilizing and destroying, larger Soviet formations in the central area. Finnish tactics evolved accordingly. With the experience they gained in the first few weeks of war, they came to resemble a mid-twentieth-century version of the French and Indians at Monongahela 185 years earlier. Soviet assault columns of tanks, artillery, and logistic support were obliged to move on the only roads and tracks available, single-line tracks through thick forest areas. These would first be brought to a halt by fire, mines, or obstacles placed in front of the columns and, to prevent any form of retreat, also at the rear. Finnish soldiers and snipers moving fast among the roadside trees on skis would then harass the immobilized column for twenty-four hours or more, shooting or throwing grenades, often homemade, at the flanks of the column as Soviet soldiers clambered in confusion out of their tanks and lorries.[1] Occasionally Finnish soldiers were able to infiltrate the Red Army vehicles, creating panic. If the bewildered Soviet soldiers decided to close down and remain in their vehicles, they suffered cold, hunger, and fatigue. Many decided to surrender after long hours of misery, enabling their attackers to move on to assault another section of the column or another column elsewhere.

The Finns called such an encircled Red Army column a *motti*, a Finnish word referring to a cubic-meter cut of wood that could be chipped at and eventually hacked to pieces. Sometimes the Finns were able to break a *motti* into several sections which could then be destroyed piecemeal, although larger columns proved more difficult in view of the shortage of Finnish manpower. The Suomi submachine gun was a major asset, referred to by Soviet soldiers as "White Death."

As the war progressed, the Red Army developed tactics to counter encirclement. From bigger columns soldiers rushed out of tanks and vehicles to build up a larger defense perimeter around an encircled column calling upon artillery support, air strikes, and a relieving column for rescue, all at times when their numerical superiority, better command, and more modern equipment were telling against the Finns. Nevertheless, the *motti* remains a remarkable addition to the skills of forest warfare, and in two important battles provided the Finns with spectacular successes.

The two battles occurred almost simultaneously, arising from the Soviet aim to cut Finland in two, with twin offensives, one north of Lake

Fig. 8.1. Remains of an ambushed Soviet column north of Suomussalmi Village.
(Courtesy of the General Headquarters, Finnish Army)

Ladoga and the second in the central "waist" of Finland using a total of some forty-eight thousand men. On 12 December a Finnish brigade-size formation under Colonel Paavo Talvela first blocked the advance of, and after a frontal attack destroyed, the Soviet 139th Division near Tolvajärus in three days of fighting; at the same time he blocked the advance of a second Soviet division, the 155th, at Ilmantsi; and, finally, by a flank attack from roadside woods, he forced a third Soviet formation, the 75th Division, to retreat in disorder. Even more spectacular was the success of Colonel Hjalmar Siilasvuo in the central "waist" of the Suomussalmi area. Here a force, which after reinforcement reached the size of a small division, first cut off the two forest roads on which the Soviet 163rd Division was advancing on Suomussalmi, and then in two weeks destroyed it. Colonel Siilasvuo then turned to a relieving 44th Division which had unwisely halted and stretched out along the southern approach road to Suomussalmi. With the road blocked at both ends, the division's columns formed perfect *mottis* for attack from the forests, and even when the Soviet tanks attempted to deal with their attackers, the Finns could retire into the depths of the forest. By early January the Soviet division had been broken up. Siilasvuo was then ordered to the south of the "waist," the Kuhmo area, where the Soviet 54th Division, although stretched out along a road, had prepared dug-in defenses. Attacking on 28 January the Finns were able to cut the road at the rear and split the division into three *mottis;* however, lacking anything other than light artillery and in face of Soviet relief forces and air supply to the encircled divisions, Siilasvuo was unable to match the complete success of Suomussalmi. He succeeded, however, in containing the Soviet division and harassing the *mottis* until the end of the war in March.[2] In all the battles the Finns captured much useful Red Army weaponry and stores which, put to good use, enabled them to continue fighting as long as they did—thereby securing a healthy Soviet respect which spared them the fate of Estonia, Latvia, and Lithuania.

In the May–June 1940 campaign in France, the Germans took advantage of the woods of the Ardennes to conceal some of General Heinz Guderian's attacking units that were later to break through so dramatically. German tanks had trained before the war in the Black Forest. Columns of tanks were led through the trees by a staff car with a metal bar, the length equaling the width of a tank, fastened to the front bumper. The Germans were, of course, assisted by the fact that French intelligence and reconnaissance were looking in the wrong direction, and also by Marshal Pétain's belief, from the 1920s on, that the Ardennes were impassable. The remainder of the campaign, however, took place in more open country with only occasional fighting around, rather than in, wooded areas.

THE GERMAN INVASION OF THE SOVIET UNION

The Germans invaded the Soviet Union on 22 June 1941, opening the largest campaign involving forests since Napoleon's invasion. Their millions of soldiers required vast stretches in which to maneuver, and within several areas of this space there were large forest belts running north to south, some adjacent to swamps.[3] Moreover this terrain, a natural barrier for any invader of the Russian heartland, was one in which an invader with inferior-sized armies had to maintain movement and momentum or face the piecemeal erosion of its formations. But because the great size of some of the forest and swamp areas made it unwise to bypass them, pockets of resistance would remain and the momentum would stall. These pockets could be as large as several divisions in size and could remain far behind the forward tanks, well concealed deep in the forests. Other geological factors assisted the Soviet defense but were later to be an impediment when the Red Army returned to the attack. The lines of rivers, the autumn and spring mud, and the extreme cold of the Russian winter would later wreak havoc on the Red Army when it entered the Carpathians and the northern Balkans.

In the northern sector, facing German attempts to take Leningrad, were woodlands and large swamp areas, all ill-suited for fast moving Panzer formations. The central area was even more difficult territory. The Orsha Corridor between large forest areas of birch or conifer with dense undergrowth offered the quickest route to Moscow, but approaching the Corridor was hindered by the Pripet marshes, and nearer Moscow lay a belt of birch woods in both the north and central areas. Roaming packs of wolves added to the gloom of the dense trees. The southern sector was relatively easier to traverse, as forests gave way to open steppes. Improvised strategic roads, which the Germans referred to as *Rollbahnen,* were constructed by their military engineers, often on existing tracks and generally dead straight for many miles and, when necessary, built on embankments to surmount swamps. But these, and forests on either side of them, channeled any fast moving armored thrusts along their lengths, making them targets for Soviet artillery and, later, partisans. Foot or horse-drawn units had frequently to be

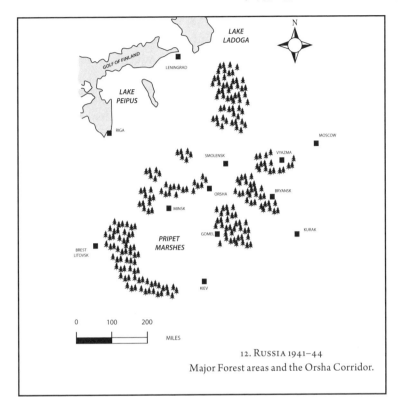

12. RUSSIA 1941–44
Major Forest areas and the Orsha Corridor.

denied the use of the *Rollbahnen* to avoid congestion and reduce the wear and tear in conditions of dust or mud. Until other roads or tracks were opened up, if that had been possible, infantry had to move through forest paths, hazardous at the best of times, exhausting and ever more dangerous as partisans became organized and active.

Very different from the meticulous planning of the May–June 1940 assault on France, German planning for the invasion of the Soviet Union was poor. Too much was based on Hitler's overconfidence that the Soviet Union would quickly collapse following attacks by a concentration of swiftly moving armored formations on a few economic and strategic areas, at the outset Ukraine and Leningrad and later Moscow. The Germans emulated Napoleon's summer campaign strategy only to bring about the same disastrous results at the hands of an army that excelled in winter. No thought was given to a more protracted a campaign involving forests and swamps, autumn and late spring mud, heavy rain and snow, extreme cold rendering weapons and equipments unusable, and short winter days. Instinctively German commanders hated forests, especially in the half-light of winter. Only a very few army, corps, or division generals gave thought to the terrain, and topographical and tactical intelligence was lacking or misleading. Very few units had even rudimentary theater training, and regiments brought in later from France or Italy had none at all. German vehicles, logistic or armored, had a low ground clearance and were to sink into the mud in spring and autumn, making even the best roads impassable; the Red Army's vehicles had higher ground clearance. Soviet expertise also extended to the rapid building by field engineers of secure wooden bridges with sharp-nosed, wedge-shaped substructure ice fenders to prevent crushing by ice floes in the big river or by floating river bridges. German wooden bridges were often swept away by the force of water, mud, or ice.

At the outset German armored formations, large and unwieldy, would rapidly bypass woods or forests through gaps, the Orsha in particular, to maintain momentum, hugging roads or tracks. The Soviet formations and units outflanked or left behind would withdraw into the woods and forests on either side of the road or track, their smaller size making for agility. From there they might emerge later and from the flank, launching a surprise attack against German infantry that had been following behind the armor, regrouping, or simply resting. The Germans would be forced to abandon their lorries and embark on long, fatiguing, and dangerous marches. Lengths of road through forests became lined with Germans, dead or dying. A strong German column might opt for a counterattack, only to the find that the Soviets would again withdraw into the roadside forests where the Germans, with insufficient manpower, were unable to pursue them. Soviet forces engaged in these operations might include regiments with Siberian experience, Cossacks, and in winter ski troops. When such Soviet harassment or combats were successful, quantities of abandoned German equipment would be handed over to partisans. Captured Germans were lucky if they were not shot or hung. As a consequence, German infantry had to be taken from forward units to be deployed on the flanks of roads or tracks to secure safe transit.

On the occasions when German infantry was ordered into the woods to clear out the forests they fared little better. Advancing in groups of twelve to twenty rather than in a line, they would soon lose cohesion, become lost, and split up into isolated pairs or threesomes. Shouted orders only added to the confusion. Unit officers had to be up front with their soldiers to retain command, but they soon were targeted. The forest edges would become dangerous, being known targets for Soviet artillery. The Soviet defenders in the forest would retire deep into the interior gloom, with well-fortified earth and timber defense works protected by wire and mines. They would withhold fire until the last minute to achieve the element of surprise. If they withdrew, attackers would encounter booby traps. In scores of local battles, the losers, German or Soviet, would seek safety in a wood, a safety often short-lived.

In one early battle, on 26 July 1941 at Prozhany, a whole German division had to be deployed to clear the road from Slonim to Minsk which had been blocked by a Soviet formation that had emerged from forests on either side of the road. Using heavy machine guns, the Germans drove the Soviets back into the trees, but they limited their entry into the forests in numbers sufficient only to protect the roads.

The Soviet soldier was generally physically more robust and "at home" in forests than the Germans, more able to move across terrain the Germans considered impassable. He was able to use local horses stronger than those of the Germans, and could commandeer light farm and forest wagons. Local "know how" led the Soviet signalers to insert ground rods into wet forest soil; these could detect currents from German line systems.

In October 1941 the Germans adopted a successful reprisal tactic in the Kletnya area, near Bryansk. Here the German LIII Infantry Corps, which had been bypassed by forward armored units, found itself threatened by Soviet forces equivalent to three divisions. The area was thickly forested and swampy, one part of it including a stretch of a *Rollbahn*. The corps commander decided to seal off the whole area using three combat battalions and two battalions of construction engineers. These detachments then set to work, defending themselves when necessary. Every stretch of dry ground around the edges of the forest swamp was blocked with obstacles and mines, and the area around the German-controlled road was blocked with a triple mine belt. In all, some forty thousand mines were laid. Attacks by the Soviets quickly became bogged down in the minefields and repulsed, allowing the main German drive toward Bryansk to be maintained. Another German success occurred near Gomel in the autumn of 1941, when the Soviets attempted to build a continuous line of strong points across the thickest part of a local forest. Disabled Soviet tanks had been dug in to provide mutual fire support. The advancing Germans met with fierce fire from dense undergrowth, but they managed to bring up antitank weapons to knock out the dug-in tanks so that small groups of infantry were then able to deal with the survivors from the Soviet strong points.

Initially the Germans placed great faith in artillery and multi-barreled rocket launchers in forest operations, not fully aware of the many practical difficulties presented by guns in forests even if the forest permitted their movement and use. Survey personnel had to have time to plot gun positions, but artillery support, if it was to be effective, had to be prompt. This seldom could be the case. Forward observation officers had to use radio, not always reliable in forests, rather than wire, and had to be very well trained. If that were the case, it was possible to coordinate the fire of a whole regiment on a single target obstructing an advance. But such coordination, and the wider coordination of artillery fire and advancing infantry, was almost impossible to arrange quickly in woods. The Germans soon came to prefer small mortar teams that required fewer men and provided simpler if more rudimentary fire control; also, because the mortars were carried by hand, teams were able to move around more easily in forest conditions. The Red Army used direct artillery fire in forests to good effect, but it, too, came to see that mortars were easier to move around—and easier to produce.

Some German commanders favored the use of a single tank or a small number moving along forest tracks in support of infantry; even if the head tank was held up or damaged, it might still be able to provide fire support. Other commanders saw nothing but the loss of tanks, if not stuck in snow or mud then destroyed in an ambush. The Soviets were more enterprising; their tanks, notably the T 34/75, with a higher ground clearance than the German tanks and a very powerful engine, could frequently be used in forests. Red Army horse cavalry was also used in regiments or in larger strengths in winter to attack or harass German rear formations and installations when the terrain was too difficult for other arms.

German air support for combat in forests and woods was much superior to that of the Soviets. Reconnaissance and air photography aircraft, flying low over the treetops to achieve surprise and avoid antiaircraft fire, was a major asset to German intelligence. When available, strike aircraft support was invaluable, provided the single-engine JU 87 Stuka dive bombers could identify a target area. If these areas had been spotted earlier by air reconnaissance or forward troops, and if the Stuka pilots had been meticulously briefed on indicators and timings, Stuka strikes could be highly effective. But as time passed Stuka pilots were less thoroughly trained, the Stuka aircraft itself carried no ground-to-air radio control, and inexperienced pilots failed to pick up flare, smoke, or other incendiary target markers fired by ground troops. Still, at its best, Stuka air-to-ground bombing could be as close as a hundred yards ahead of advancing attackers and, unless the Soviet soldiers were well entrenched, could inflict heavy casualties. The Stuka, too, wherever it was used, also carried with it a psychological factor: the terrifying screech of specially fitted sirens on the aircraft's undercarriage, the *Jericho-Trompete* (in later models the sirens were removed and bombs with a screeching whistle were used instead). Added to the noise of exploding bombs and crashing trees, Stuka dive bombing could inspire true terror. When in the spring of 1942 a major Stuka offensive took place south of Lake Ilmen, with aircraft dropping 1,000-kg bombs into woods, the morale of Soviet soldiers was severely shaken.

Both armies used their engineers to clear, construct, and open new forest roads or to broaden forest tracks. In forests, the Germans also used engineers to construct earthworks, abattis, observation towers, and antitank obstacles and minefields.

The Red Army, in addition to the general problems of morale and discipline within any army in a brutal war, had a domestic problem arising from the cruelties and excesses of Stalin in the 1930s. Some conscripts could not bring themselves to fight for the regime with any great enthusiasm, particularly at the outset and in some of the non-Russian regions. If identified, malcontents and criminals were used by the Soviets in penal units as decoys.[4]

The remaining enormously important feature of forest fighting in the Soviet-German campaigns was the use of partisans, most frequently operating from forests in the north and central areas. Soviet partisan activity began as early as July 1941, and by 1944 more than two hundred thousand partisans , if not more, were at their most active in winter. Huge areas of the Soviet Union were, in effect, under brutal partisan control. They were acclaimed as the "Fourth Army" by the Soviet political and military leadership; to the Germans they were a festering, ever spreading cancer.

The first partisans were mostly Soviet soldiers who had been cut off by the speed of the German armor advance, some escaping from encirclement. Others were deserters or local men and a growing number of women. Initially they used captured or abandoned German weapons. A clandestine conscription was soon applied in areas unsupervised by the Germans. Men were funneled out of forests in special secured corridors and given training, weapons, and equipment before being returned to action. Strict military and political discipline was applied; partisans fighting for a free Ukraine or any cause other than the Soviet Union and its communist leadership were eliminated. Soviet aircraft dropped ammunition, food, medical supplies, and in winter warm clothing; in the cold months partisans built wooden encampments concealed among trees. As well as sabotage, the task of intelligence gathering was given high priority to partisans. Military liaison and political officers served alongside partisan groups, and either they or trusted partisan leaders were sent operational instructions by radio. Partisan operations and welfare were always subordinated, no matter the cost in partisan lives, to the interests of the formal Red Army formations in the area, even extending to the use of partisan groups as decoys to save the lives of soldiers.

The "Forest Brotherhood" partisan became an iconic hero figure in the Soviet Union's war image, with its special appeal to patriotism but also as an excellent example of Marxist teachings on the unity of front and rear in the common revolutionary cause as well as other wider political propaganda.[5]

Fig. 8.2. Soviet soldiers preparing to blow up a railway line behind German lines.
(Courtesy of the Russian Army)

German accounts set out the security efforts that the Germans were obliged to take against partisans. All rear facilities, railway lines, centers, airfields, and ammunition and supply paths had to be guarded; even then railway lines and bridges would be blown up almost continuously, with a wearying effect on the morale and decision making of German commanders.[6] Before the crucial June 1943 German Kursk offensive, partisans blew up a vital bridge at Bryansk and disrupted the important Roslavl-Bryansk railway line. Frequently night traffic on important lines through forest areas had to be shut down despite security patrols, particularly before any German offensives. Considerable numbers of men had to be taken from frontline units for rear security duties. When, in 1943, Germans began to withdraw from occupied areas, partisans anticipated the lines of withdrawal and sedulously destroyed bridges, tactics that required the Germans to detach units or subunits in advance to secure a bridge or repair one that had been blown up. The existing practice of attacking railway lines was raised to the status of "Railway War" by a proclamation in July 1943. Since some forest partisan units had by now been provided with light antiaircraft weapons, the maps of Luftwaffe pilots were marked with red circles on many areas over which pilots were instructed not to fly at any altitude below eighty-three hundred feet. After partisan operations, German reprisals were marked by extreme savagery, the burning of settlements, and the lingering torture of captives. Yet Soviet reprisals soon came to match and surpass the horrific German measures. On the railways German trains included a supply wagon filled with captured Soviet soldiers. The murky nature of forest warfare was adding its own dark contribution to the already existing visceral hatred between Teuton and Slav.

RESISTANCE GUERRILLAS

Smaller-scale guerrilla activity in or from forests also took place in Poland, Yugoslavia, and Romania, as well as by local anti-Soviet nationalists after the Soviet re-conquest of Ukraine. In Western Europe groups of French Resistance Maquis operated from woods from 1943 on, choosing remote areas on the Massif Central, the Jura, and the Pyrenees. The men were mostly of the working class with former soldiers and sailors of the Vichy government forces disbanded after the German occupation of Unoccupied France in November 1942. Most, but certainly not all, Maquisards were Communists, and coordination either locally or from London was often difficult to arrange.[7] The groups living in woods occupied several different hiding places for security, coming together only for an attack. In winter, when trees lost their foliage and Maquisards might be observed from the air, refuge was sought in farm buildings. Life in the woods, especially in cold weather, was harsh; food was limited, perhaps little more than potatoes, and clothing was inadequate. Ill health followed, especially if the local water supply was polluted, although at times wine proved an agreeable alternative. The Maquisards depended heavily on the goodwill of sympathetic locals who would leave them farm products at the edges of woods and forests. The Maquisards' targets were bridges and railways, occasionally a factory producing German war materials. A complicated and slow procedure was arranged for dropping weapons and explosives from Britain, weather permitting, by parachute or secret landings at night following requests passed on and acknowledged with coded delivery signals broadcast by the British Broadcasting Company.[8] As in the Soviet Union, by 1944 several areas were "no go" districts for the German military or the Vichy authorities Milice [[Militia] that tried to hunt them down.

NORMANDY AND ARNHEM

The fighting that followed the Allied landings in Normandy in June 1944 was mostly in high hedge *bocage* terrain or the more open country of Belgium and Holland. Small woods that concealed Germans were often identified early on by the numbers of mines dug on their fronts or by mortar fires from the wood itself. Clearing such small woods was sometimes costly in unit lives, even when supported by "Crocodiles," flame throwers mounted on Churchill tanks.

In the North-West Europe Liberation Campaign, the Battle at Arnhem, from 17 to 25 September 1944 saw fighting in thickly wooded country, particularly in the early stages. It was hoped that the seizure by parachute and airborne forces of the big road bridge over the Lower Rhine would enable the British Twenty-first Army Group to sweep rapidly into Germany, and thus quickly end the war. Unfortunately, however, the British airborne divisional commander appointed to oversee the landings decided not to accept the clear intelligence advice that the area near Arnhem chosen for the landings contained a large number of German troops. His division, one of two parachute brigades and a glider-borne aircraft-landing brigade (later joined by a small Polish brigade), accordingly landed in clearings surrounded by woods some six miles northeast of their target, at the vital bridge. Nearby were two German armored divisions, between the British landing zone and Arnhem town, between wooded country and the small suburb of Oosterbeek.

Attempting a dash from the landing zone to the town and its bridge, British units came under totally unexpected heavy German fire, particularly from tanks and armored vehicles using rocket-propelled mortar

Fig. 8.3. Arnhem, fighting in the woods.
(Courtesy of the Imperial War Museum, photo no. BU1142)

bombs. These forced two of the three battalions of the 1st Parachute Brigade off the road to take refuge in the woods. Just one battalion reached the northern end of the bridge only to find Germans at the southern end, thus opening an epic but unsuccessful battle which would last until the 28th, with relief and withdrawal operations to follow. Men of the aircraft-landing brigade were attacked in the woods by Germans, who set areas of the wood on fire to force the British out. British counterattacks led to small-scale but difficult fighting, both sides using the woods and trees for ambushes. Communications broke down, as the British field wireless sets were not suited for conditions in the woods—a circumstance anticipated by one British company commander who had trained his men to act on Peninsula War bugle calls. Failing light added to the confusion.

As a private soldier of one of the parachute battalions recalled: "During one of the encounters a German soldier emerged from the trees and one of our NCOs went to bring him in; as he did so, other Germans under cover shot him. From then on we said, 'No Prisoners' (we had nowhere to put them anyway)." A mortar platoon commander noted that his fire controller could see little of the ground ahead because of its broken nature, but he effectively searched it with bursts of rapid fire which made the enemy withdraw rapidly, leaving a truck behind.

One commander of the battalion company summed up the forest fighting:

> We kept losing people, a few here and a few there. . . .
> What happens in close country is that people have a go at this and that and you never see them again. It was a bash-bash-bash sort of business. The missing men weren't all killed or wounded. The idea is that you meet up again somewhere, but it didn't often happen.[9]

THE ARDENNES

The American Army had to fight a very grim battle in the extreme cold and snow-covered terrain of the 1944–45 winter, following the surprise of the German offensive that opened on 16 December in the woods of the Ardennes.[10] The assault involved three armies of eighteen divisions of varying quality, but the best six were equipped with a number of the most modern and powerful tanks, tank destroyers, and assault guns. In the Ardennes the Americans had only six divisions of which three were inexperienced and three recuperating after earlier fighting; none was making any particular preparations for a German offensive. The regiments that were to form the vanguard of the German attack were moved forward over three nights; by day they remained hidden in the Eifel forests preparing hot food by means of special charcoal that emitted no smoke.

Surprise and the weight of the German onslaught broke up the cohesion of many American units. Small and isolated groups attempted to hold road junctions and crossroads using roadside woods as cover for ambushes. The Germans, in turn and if conditions allowed, would enter the wood to secure the road and maintain the momentum of advance. This momentum brought the Germans in conflict, again often in woods, with American rear artillery batteries, logistic units, and parks. Only after the American command released four additional divisions, two armored and two airborne, did the fighting return to organized formations and unit combat. The engagements that followed revealed old and new problems in those encounters that took place in the woods. German horse-drawn artillery found movement on slushy paths through woods very difficult. Rocket-launched mortar bombs exploding among trees showered splinters on American soldiers in slit trenches, men already deafened by their noise. Through some of the woods American tanks were able to move slowly, but ammunition supplies had to be moved forward through the trees on sleds over the snow. In the siege of Bastogne detachments of German mixed tank and infantry subunits emerged from concealment in the surrounding small woods to harass the perimeter of American defenses. The woods of the Baraque de Freiture to the north of Bastogne also held hidden German artillery and mortar batteries bombarding the Americans. In turn, when these batteries were spotted they were attacked by American aircraft. German units caught on the road by American air attacks or attacks by superior American formations hurried into woods for safety.

By 27 December, however, Bastogne had been relieved, and the Germans had accepted that their attempt at a decisive breakthrough had failed. The German Army's last opportunity to mount an offensive that could alter the course of the war had passed in the woods of the Ardennes.

HÜRTGEN FOREST

At the same time as the Battle of Ardennes, the last month of 1944 and early 1945 were to see what can justly be claimed as the greatest single forest fight in recorded history. The battle was to last for five autumn and winter months; in it both the numbers involved and the experience developed in forest fighting were epic.

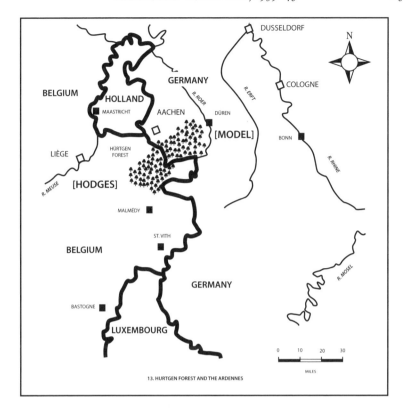

13. HURTGEN FOREST AND THE ARDENNES

The battle centered in and around the huge Hürtgen Forest, which lay just inside Germany's western frontier with Belgium, to the south of Aachen.[11] The forest was some six to ten miles wide and twenty miles long, covering hilly ground with some hills more than two thousand feet high in four ridge systems extending north, northwest, and east. Each ridge system dominated surrounding ground. Some ridge crests had been cleared; in the ravines and lower ground was some of Europe's most dense forest terrain. Much of the forest was comprised of close rows of pines, many as high as one hundred feet; these covered the ground with a thick treacherous carpet of pine needles and equally treacherous mud according to the season. Other areas recently refor-ested were planted with lower trees but had a thicker undergrowth with equivalent difficulties. A few villages lay in the clear higher ground. The Roer River ran along the eastern edge of the forest.

At the best of times, in the dark fully grown conifer areas where the treetops mingled together, the sun could only penetrate to ground level in small circular spots. The lower branches of the trees interlocked in many areas so that men had to stoop and bend to move along. Visibility was reduced generally to twenty or thirty yards, sometimes only ten.[12] One section of the forest could look very much like another, and soldiers became confused. The few roads across and through the forest were second or third class with firebreak tracks even more narrow. In autumn and winter the tracks degraded to deep slippery mud. Water, or in winter snow, dripped down from the trees continuously.

Hürtgen lay on the flank of the U.S. Army's First Army, commanded by General Courtney Hodges, in its September 1944 dash toward Cologne and Düsseldorf, an army in a hurry to finish the war by Christmas. Why Hürtgen was not bypassed and left to wither is not entirely clear, but there were fears of a flank attack from the forest falling on General Lawton Collins's advancing VIII Corps. Later, in something of a post hoc justification, it was claimed that the hope had been to capture the upstream dams on the Roer; commanders, it was said, feared that the Germans would release the water behind the dams, thereby trapping any Americans who had crossed to the opposite bank. This fear does not seem to have been expressed at the time, however. There was also a serious intelligence underestimation that the Germans had only insignificant numbers remaining in the forest. In the event, a massive "mission creep" was to follow. Over the five months from September 1944 to February 1945, clearing the forest a few yards at a time involved eight infantry and two armored divisions; America's final victory contributed little to an already successful major theater campaign.

The nature of forest terrain imposed great restrictions on the main military assets of the U.S. Army. The use of tank destroyers and tanks in the single-line firebreak tracks was very limited—and dangerous for the tanks; their main role became one of screening forest edges. Air support was also severely constrained by mist and clouds. At forest-floor level radio was often useless amid the trees and hills; antennae broke when carried among tree branches, and batteries were affected by the damp. Consequently formation commanders received little immediate operational intelligence. Mine-detection equipment was also jeopardized by the general damp conditions, the dripping water and rain—and, before long, also by shards from shell bursts falling onto the ground. Some mines had been constructed with glass to evade metal-detection equipment. Undergrowth or wood everywhere precluded getting any vehicles to the frontline soldiers; other soldiers had to be detached from combat units to act as porters. Casualty evacuation was equally difficult, if not impossible, and frequently the bodies of the dead, torn and bloody, had to be left where they had fallen. Some were later fitted with booby traps by the Germans, clearly dampening the morale of the next American attacking units. Many presumed dead were never accounted for. Lines of the engineers' white tape, sometimes as long as three thousand feet, often had to be laid to guide supply and medical personnel in and out of the forest, but these were liable to be swept away by wind or shell fire.

The newly arrived Americans knew little or nothing of these terrain hazards. The Germans did, however, and took full advantage of them; their West Wall line of defense lay right through the Hürtgen. On the approach roads were several rows of concrete antitank obstacles, five-foot-high "dragons' teeth," together with mines and supported by pillboxes with machine guns and antitank weaponry. The firebreak forest tracks were mined, not only along the track itself but also along the sides to catch tank crews forced to leave their machines. Within the forest the Americans' first obstacle was a barbed-wire barrage, twenty-five yards deep in some zones and laced with mines and booby traps. These had to be cleared under fire with the additional hazard that the American mine detectors could not detect the light antipersonnel mines—mines that inflicted physical and psychological wounds more often than fatalities, although many deaths occurred as well.. Later in the long battle the Americans learned to cover these mines with metal meshing to indicate their location and warn following units, and the Germans learned to cover them with booby-trapped tree branches.[13] Behind the barbed wire lay clusters cantered around old Siegfried Line constructions, namely, command post blockhouses with walls and roofs protected by several feet of concrete covered by logs and dirt for additional strength and camouflage. Within the cluster there would also be a rebuilt command post and a small medical aid post; around the cluster would be a network of trenches, snipers in slits, log bunkers, and antitank and mortar pits,

Fig. 8.4. Fighting in Hürtgen Forest.
(Courtesy of the U.S. Army Military History Institute)

all with interlocking plans for field- or machine-gun attacks. In some areas "tunnels of fire," difficult for an attacker to spot, would be prepared by cutting down lower middle-level tree branches. Some snipers, equipped with rifles with telescopic sights, were lodged in camouflaged hideouts high up in other branches. On the forest tracks the powerful Teller antitank mines were laid in groups of three, carefully spaced to deceive engineers that had located the fire into believing that the track was now clear. Besides knocking out one or several tanks, the resulting delay would disrupt or destroy entirely the plans of follow-up infantry. Fallen trees were also used to block tank advances along narrow firebreaks. The villages in the forest clearing had to be taken in costly hand-to-hand fighting.

The German defense most feared by the Americans, however, was the German artillery, namely, their 105-mm howitzers and 88-mm guns, their fire perhaps supported by mortars and occasionally directed by spotter aircraft. Such a barrage would unfold, particularly in the early months, according to a prearranged fire plan designed to move forward and back over an American advance or to channel advancing Americans into specific clearer areas to be fully bombarded later. Shells from the guns would explode in the treetops, shards of shell splinters and woods falling down on infantrymen with devastating effect, particularly if soldiers crouched low, exposing more of their bodies. Soldiers were told to "hug a tree" for body protection, their heads protected by their helmets.[14] German artillery fire would also destroy line telephone tracks between headquarters and units. German defense was often proactive as well, with dazed and confused Americans the target of a full-force German bayonet charge or German air attack dropping the light and difficult to defuse "Butterfly" antipersonnel bomb, sometimes with the support of the few tanks available to the Germans moving down a fire-break. One exception was the major German air attack on 3 December involving sixty aircraft, which failed to kill a single American soldier but cost the Luftwaffe nineteen aircraft. Detachments of Germans would remain concealed among the trees, allowing the Americans to bypass them, and then they would later emerge to attack supply and communication lines. To the American soldier, Hürtgen Forest became known as the "Death Machine."

The order of battle of the German defense centered initially around three under-strength and ill-equipped divisions, joined later by other divisions and regiments that came to hand, some cobbled together with survivors from previous battles.[15] Most were short of officers. Some regiments were made up of middle-aged or elderly men, for example, a section of the erstwhile Parisian garrison that must have found the changing life scene very difficult. The personnel of other regiments varied from a few good professionals to local home defense groups, sailors and Luftwaffe ground staff. At least one unit was comprised of anti-Soviet Russians, prisoners of war led by German officers. Anyone who wavered was punished; deserters, if caught, were hung. At the outset certain Nazi Party chieftains—known as *grosse Tiere*, or "big beasts," came to exhort and threaten them. In general, most fought because they had no alternative and also wanted to defend their homeland. Among the younger soldiers were fanatic Nazi supporters who fought for their ideological beliefs, but many of the older men and veterans of the Normandy campaign believed that, whatever the outcome in the forest, the war was lost. They were all commanded by the redoubtable Field Marshal Walter Model, a soldier known for his absolute ruthlessness. After the end of the battle on 21 April, Model, in the tradition of Varus and Samsonov, committed suicide to avoid blame for his failure and also, with good reason, to avoid being handed over to the Soviets.

The first American attacks, those of the 3rd Armored Division beginning of 12 September, the 9th Infantry Division late in September and October, and the 28th Infantry Division in early November, faced increasing difficulties, some units suffering casualties as high as 50 percent. Many regiments had performed very well in Normandy, but they were in no way prepared for dense forest fighting. There were no reliable maps; unit officers relied on compass bearings. Fairly quickly the importance of artillery and mortars was appreciated, particularly infantrymen following a creeping barrage. But amid the trees the infantry suffered severely. Command of any body of men larger than a platoon was impossible. Extended line advance soon led to confusion and cohesion was lost, especially when German snipers targeted officers and NCOs, many of whom were killed or wounded. If a soldier left a slit trench or dugout he could very quickly lose all sense of direction. Commanders had to urge men on to maintain the momentum of their advance; otherwise soldiers might simply seek refuge from German artillery.

Tactics for dealing with the blockhouses and bunkers were soon worked out. Some commanders preferred to attack at dusk or night-time. Attacks would open with a light artillery, with fighter bombers and mortar bombardments seeking to eliminate any defenders in foxholes or trenches around the blockhouse. But target identification was difficult, almost impossible, for aircraft. If no heavier weaponry was at hand, a rifle party would fire continuously at the blockhouse. Then the weapon slits of the blockhouse would be targeted, by a tank if available, if not by men creeping among the trees and through any undergrowth to try to drop grenades through the slits. Finally, an infantry section or sections would close to finish off any survivors. Sometimes mines or other explosive charges would be placed on the roof of a bunker or against a side wall; on other occasions flame throwers or antitank grenade launchers would be needed. On the few occasions that the ground permitted small groups of tanks to operate and immediate radio communication was possible, infantry platoon commanders would ride into battle on the hull of a tank and command their sections by radio.

The next series of attacks, those made by the 1st, 4th, 8th, 9th, 75th, and 83rd Infantry Divisions, were to suffer severely from late autumn rain, with the additional burden of their clothing becoming permanently cold and wet. In the exceptionally cold December winter, temperatures fell to -40 degrees centigrade. A single blanket was poor cover and any form of camp or cooking fire had to be forbidden. Casualties due to hypothermia, lung ailments, trench foot, and sheer exhaustion mounted. There were also a growing number of self-inflicted or buddy-inflicted wounds. As time passed, areas of the forest became littered with corpses of men who had either died on the spot or could not be evacuated, and human remains and clothing hanging from tree branches and from burned-out vehicles and tanks.

The prolonged battle once more exposed a weakness, one already noted, in the U.S. Army's unit reinforcement procedure. Except for the major attack, for example, that of November 1944 when ten divisions were in the area, one or two divisions would be kept in the forest for two weeks before a period of relief. In rest periods for the other divisions, casualties would be replaced and then in turn returned to the forest. This procedure carried particular disadvantages in forest warfare with its loss of cohesion. Surviving soldiers would find themselves in small, perhaps two-man "buddy-buddy" teams with men they did not know whose training was inadequate and whom they were not certain they could trust.[16] Exhausted, cold, hungry, and too often isolated in the Hürtgen's eerie gloom, morale would collapse in units and individuals would crack under all the pressure. Very large numbers of men had to be withdrawn from the forest because of "fatigue" or "trench foot." There was also much resentment among the men, not always justified, that neither middle-level regimental nor more senior officers were to be seen visiting the forest positions. A number of soldiers are believed to have sought death rather than continue in the fighting. For others, both Americans and Germans, the fight in the forest became a one-dimensional fact of life: nothing mattered other than a singularly concentrated view of killing the adversary. Such thinking, of course, occurred in other battles, but the confines and darkness of the trees and forest clearly exacerbated tension, giving it exceptional force on the local theater stage.

Finally, two massive offensives launched in icy wind and snow between 8 and 10 February involving divisions from the American Ninth Army and other Allied troops added to the Germans' difficulties to the north of the forest and at last cleared the area. Both offensives were preceded by very heavy artillery and air-to-ground strikes in the forest and surrounding areas, reducing large stretches of the forest to tree stumps.

Figures for casualties at Hürtgen have been assessed at as high as twenty-three thousand killed or wounded and another nine thousand incapacitated. Both at the time and for some time afterward American historians and commanders' autobiographies have tended to draw a veil over Hürtgen, perhaps because, despite the tenacity of the American frontline soldiers in the several divisions, the whole Hürtgen battle proved so difficult and prolonged for its commanders. However hard and bravely soldiers may have fought, glory is not immediately evident in a slow-moving forest battle.

THE VOSGES AND THE BLACK FOREST

At the same time as the Hürtgen Forest battle, and on the extreme right of the Allied armies crossing France into Germany, General Jean de Lattre de Tassigny's French First Army had landed on the Mediterranean coast and were advancing up the Rhone. The French Army became heavily involved in extreme cold winter fighting in the small valleys of the Vosges and the woods in Alsace, and later, after entering Germany, in the woods and forests of the Black Forest. The Alsace fighting was especially severe, but by March and April 1945 German resistance in the Black Forest had been severely weakened both in strength and enthusiasm. The French divisions had included Zonaves and a Foreign Legion regiment, Algerian and Moroccan Tirailleurs infantry, Moroccan and

Algerian Spahis light-cavalry horsemen, as well as former Free French units and others formed from resistance groups. The pattern of fighting in Alsace involved much forest patrolling, combing, and clearing, in which the North African Spahis excelled, and, later in Germany, attempts by the Germans to harass the advancing French armored columns by attacking from roadside woods. The Germans also turned to building traditional pine-wood abattis to stop French columns on country roads or forest tracks, thus providing targets for their mortar or artillery fire. The campaign ended with sweeps through the woods on the slopes of the Voralberg by Moroccan infantry and wild irregular Goumiers, company-sized units made up of horse and foot soldiers recruited in Morocco's Atlas Mountains.[17]

9

Post-1945
AND
Conclusion

SINCE THE END OF THE SECOND World War little combat in woods and forests has taken place in Europe and none in North America. Such combat was, however, often the subject of theory and exercise by cold war military commanders. Actual combat on a relatively small scale took place first in Greece from 1945 to 1948, in which communist partisans of the National People's Liberation Army made use of woods in the mountain areas, and, forty-five years later, in the conflict following the collapse of Yugoslavia. In Croatia, Bosnia, and Kosovo ethnic guerrilla units or bands used forests as bases. In the long Northern Ireland campaign British Special Forces would track and hunt down Irish nationalist groups in the border woods. On a larger scale, in an area on the extreme edge of Europe, forest fighting followed the collapse of the Soviet Union and the Chechen insurgency. In Vietnam the U.S. Army engaged in some forest fighting similar to that in earlier European combat.

During the long cold war, confrontation between the land and air forces of the North Atlantic Treaty Organization (NATO) and the Warsaw Pact forces on the inner German border between West and East Germany, led to much theoretical writing and study. Massive military forces would be stationed on each side of the border. The Soviet and Warsaw Pact forces, composed essentially of shock armored and mechanized infantry formations, were planning for fast-moving strategic breakthroughs in which forest areas were to be bypassed in a dash for the Rhine and the English Channel. Both sides saw forests as having subsidiary use in such a campaign. NATO planning for a Soviet attack appreciated that certain woods and forests, while providing concealment and thick cover, would also channel the Soviets' advance along particular routes, slowing momentum which would perhaps lead to congestion and thus enable a hammer-and-anvil defense plan. The NATO plan also provided for parties to remain behind in woods after a Soviet Army advance, observing the movements of Soviet second-echelon formations and reporting to NATO headquarters by means of short-burst signal systems. Soviet planning, particularly in the last two decades of the cold war, was more ambitious, reflecting Soviet thinking on maneuver warfare, itself much influenced by Marxist concepts of the essential unity of front and rear. Special Forces units and subunits were to land behind NATO lines and, after assembling, move out from woods and forests to strike at NATO lines of communication, headquarters, ordinance parks, airfields and airstrips, and radar installations, thereby paralyzing NATO forward units. Helicopter developments in the 1970s and 1980s offered new opportunities for battlefield mobility; helicopters could provide not only for the safe bypassing of forests but also for rapid surprise lifts and troop insertions, thereby using forests and woods to a unit's advantage in either attack or defense.[1] Fortunately all these plans remained on paper.

CHECHNYA

Secessionism in the small autonomous north Caucasus republic of Chechnya led to two Russian campaigns, the first from 1994 to 1996 and the second beginning in 1999 and, in a much reduced form, continuing at the time of this writing. Of Chechnya's land area, totaling some one hundred by eighty kilometers, about 11 percent is comprised of medium-high mountain and 8 percent of high mountains. The area of medium height is heavily forested particularly over the slopes facing north, with beech forests, oak, elders, and hornbeam.[2] In the first Chechen war, after Russia's violent "shock and awe" campaign had flattened Chechnya's capital city of Grozny and cleared the lower areas of Chechnya, the insurgents withdrew to the higher ground in the south and its sixty-mile-long border with independent Georgia. The forested mountain areas with the two Argun rivers provide a route of entry into Chechnya both for supplies and foreign volunteers, such as Saudi Arabian Wahabis, Uzbekhs, Somalis, and others. In times of difficulty the forests could also serve as a route for any hard-pressed insurgent band to escape into safety. Road transport in these areas is, at best, difficult and dangerous because of limited visibility; at times, especially in the rainy season, vehicle movement is impossible. In the nineteenth century the tsar's army had cut open some swathes of forest to provide fields of fire and some protection against ambushes. The Russians tried to follow their forebears' tactics, together with helicopter logistic supply support for outposts and border posts.

In both Chechen wars the Russians experienced great difficulty in flying helicopters in the forest *rayons.* Wind conditions could vary greatly and suddenly both in direction and strength, making landings hazardous and any use of helicopters as gunships quite uncertain. In the first conflict the Russians sought to extend shock and awe, and the destruction of villages on the edges of the forests, by positioning artillery at the actual edge and firing into the forest while dropping random bombs at the same time. Some of the bombs and shells were new, highly destructive, tactical-level, thermobasic, or fuel-air explosives. In their occasional forays into the forest, poorly prepared Russian soldiers were more concerned with preserving their own lives than with attacking their opponents; the forays achieved little. The Chechen insurgents, supported by well-publicized foreign Muslim volunteers often of little military value, would then withdraw further into the forests, trying to lure the Russians into pursuit to then ambush them from all sides. Some insurgent bands either lived entirely in the woods or found shelter in remote forest villages, emerging to strike at Russian posts or headquarters. Russians initially remained prudent in the use of helicopters, keeping them airborne. One reason for this caution was the sharp differences of opinion on how, or even whether, the war should be fought and which of the many rival government services and agencies should be in charge. These differences eventually led to a cease-fire and the end of the first war.

In the second war the Russians and their Chechen collaborators again saw their priority as taking control of Grozny and the lower ground areas, hoping that, by so doing, resistance would continue for only a short time in the mountains and forests. Russian forces were by now better equipped and trained with much greater gun, mortar, and rocket-launcher firepower which they planned to use at maximum range. Artillery or mortar batteries were attached to company-level sub-units in all areas. With the aim of securing their approved Chechen leaders' power; the Russians again launched a heavy assault on Grozny, flattening the capital city and its surrounding suburbs and towns, the areas of economic importance. Included in these assaults were units equipped with the Buratino, a 36-barreled rocket launcher capable of firing incendiary or fuel-air explosives and laser-guided projectiles from their 220-mm mortars.[3] Having devastated the low country, the Russians moved to more proactive incursions into the forest areas in the south, particularly in the Shatovski *rayons*. The incursions mostly took the form of raids mounted from the forest edges preceded by artillery shelling and aircraft bombing; pursuit groups with flame throwers would seek to encircle forest bands. The Russians admitted, however, that many escaped.

Other groups were landed by helicopter in small village areas or small open clearings deep in the southern mountain forests. These groups were usually Special Forces rather than line infantry and were to meet unexpected hazards. The Russians have been reticent and have not released a full account of all the practical difficulties these missions experienced, but accounts of two disasters and other press reports provide some insight.

The first disaster occurred at the end of February 2000, when airborne solders of a Parachute *Desyant* Company were massacred in or following a helicopter landing on a forest-covered hill near Ulus Kert. The second occurred in April 2007, when an HIP MI-8 helicopter carrying men of the 22nd Spetsnez Military Intelligence Brigade crashed near Sanoy, killing all the men aboard. The brigade had been called to help units already on the ground who were in pursuit of an insurgent group but had become bogged down in mud. The Russian HIP helicopters were old, most twenty-five years old or more, with reduced rotor thrust and other control problems. Further, in the HIP and other Russian helicopters the pilot's range of vision was limited to the front, making landings in windy conditions in small tree-lined spaces very dangerous indeed. Between 19 August 2002 and 27 April 2007 a total of eighteen helicopters were lost in Chechnya, seven by fire from the ground, three by crashing into a mountain, and the remainder by technical problems or pilot error causing rotor blades to hit treetops. But as the Russian pursuit attacks became progressively more effective, Chechen forest and mountain resistance fell. The strategy of opposition changed to one of sporadic attacks in Russia and the neighboring autonomous republics. The death of the leading Chechen guerrilla leader led to a nominal cease-fire and the installation of a client regime. The Russians, however, have not yet, at the time of this writing in early 2010, been able to extinguish all resistance, a resistance that still maintains its propaganda appeal in the Muslim world. In Russia itself the small number of casualties per month continues to arouse criticism, and on a remote forest-lined stretch of the Moscow–St. Petersburg railway, North Caucasian insurgents blew up the prestigious Nevsky Express train in November 2009, killing twenty-six people and wounding at least a hundred.

CONCLUSION

The encounters and battles described in these chapters suggest that forest warfare can carry with it its own particular psychological dimensions of surprise and shock, especially in the gloomy, haunting, dark setting of a dense mature forest. Fighting may then become close-quarter with a sudden attack from a flank or other defensive tricks such as ambushes, concealed pitfalls, or booby-trapped fallen trees, all considered to be "underhand" as opposed to an "honest" front engagement. These conditions can produce both the best and worst in the fighting man. At best, as, for example, with the Americans in Hürtgen Forest, soldiers may manifest a grim tenacious determination, despite all the military and terrain frustrations, taking on an attitude, for instance, that "this is a battle that must be won" or "every inch of the forest must be held." At worst, however, whether among the French Canadians and the Indians at Monongahela or the Soviet partisans and their German pursuers in the Second World War, this book shows that there can be a primeval ferocity turning to extreme cruelty in forest fighting that is not generally seen on more open battlefields. Perhaps only close-quarter street fighting carries with it the same measure of this ferocity.

Sometimes, however, the greatness and the mystery of a vast forest can lead some men to reflect philosophically on themselves, their identities, and their roles as human beings. As Lieutenant Wolfgang Paul of the German Army, commenting on his service in the Soviet Union in the winter of 1941, reflected:

> I possessed an instinct for survival in dangerous action where life and death always hang by a thread. But I could not find any understanding of this brutal war. The landscape in which our men lived and died—where death came quickly and very often—remained a mystery to me . . . I felt a deep sense of the land around me.[4]

Another view was that of the theologian Teilhard de Chardin serving at Verdun as a stretcher bearer. For him it was a return to Christ that was the only possible theme for any memorial monument: "Only the figure of Christ can draw together, express, and console what horror, hope, and profound mystery there is in such an unleashing of struggle and horror."[5] Siegfried Sassoon, watching the arrival of the 38th Division at Mametz, also wrote of the pathos of forest warfare:

> Visualizing the forlorn crowd of khaki figures under the twilight of the trees I can believe that I saw then, for the first time, how blindly war destroys its victims. The sun had gone down on my own reckless brandishings, and [I] understood the doomed condition of these half-trained civilians who had been set up to attack the wood.[6]

A study of forest warfare can be as much a study of man's wider reactions and thinking as of military history.

Traditional forest-based guerrilla fighting is likely to continue in the future, though more likely in Asia, Africa, and South America than in Europe or North America, and sometimes as much for media propaganda as for military gain. In any area in any continent, however, regular military commanders are likely, by preference, to continue to avoid forests. But the mystery of the forest may now be reduced for a modern professional army, whether involved in guerrilla fighting or international war. Today intelligence can be gathered far more efficiently than by a man with a pair of binoculars hiding behind a tree. The surprise value of an attack mounted from concealment in a wood or forest may have gone by the wayside with the introduction and use of radar and heat-detection infra-red equipment in aircraft, drones, or armored vehicles, although a well-equipped defender may have recourse to paints or uniform and camouflage fabrics that do not reflect radar and absorb infra-red emissions. Poisonous defoliants in long-range, rocket-assisted projectiles launched from ships or aircraft can destroy a forest and any tracks within it. Other chemicals, such as napalm, despite its short life, can wipe out defenders in green forest areas. Fast-moving armored assault units will once again be programmed to bypass forests or to preempt any defense of them by a task force arriving by helicopter before the defense can even be prepared. As at Hürtgen, if tanks or other armored vehicles attempt to pass through a forest area after bulldozers had tried to clear a path, the pileup of vegetation that would result would create a new and almost certainly impassable barrier. If tactical nuclear weapons were used in a conflict, they would certainly create a variety of ground-zero obstacles and radiation difficulties that would help neither attacker nor defender.

For professional soldiers this book would suggest that if, in one form or another, forest warfare does continue, so, too, would continue the two special demands that forest warfare makes on any army involved in it. The first will always fall upon the infantry whose soldiers will have to bear the brunt of the fighting, however difficult and dangerous. They deserve special training and soundly planned backup. The second demand, echoing down the forest tracks of history, is topographical intelligence without which the fighting will bring misfortune. The intelligence needed ranges from preliminary general accounts to up-to-the-minute detailed ground data collected from records, reconnaissance, air observation, and any available local sources—to be collated, analyzed, and swiftly disseminated by trained intelligence staff.

It is more likely, however, that future clashes involving forests will not be in the form of formal military combat. Any clashes by non-state actors in Asia, Africa, and South America will arise from rival local economic, commercial, and resource exploitation involving the very survival of forest areas against the demand of commerce and housing. As Arnold Zweig noted at Verdun in 1916, the actions of man can very quickly undo the work of nature over generations,[7] but in the future the trees may not be permitted to regrow, as Michael Mott's poetic lines, in the epigraph to this book, recorded that they could at Spotsylvania.

NOTES

1. INTRODUCTION

1. The absence of any forest warfare training is a recurring theme in this book. A remark that appeared in a history of a First World War division is typical of many: "When the division later went into battle, it was faced with a large, heavily defended wood but woodland fighting, despite the wooded nature of the Somme countryside, had not been included in the training programme." Colin Hughes, *Mametz: Lloyd George's Welsh Army at the Battle of the Somme* (Norwich, UK: Gliddon Books, 1990), p. 60. Hughes based this comment on an interview with a Mametz survivor.

2. Readers may find it useful to bear some figures in mind. A young plantation forest may have thousands of saplings per hectare (2.47 acres) with much undergrowth. An old oak forest may have as few as fifteen trees per hectare but each with a trunk girth of more than twenty feet or more, together with a ground littered with rotten stumps and much less undergrowth. Either of these—and many others with varying shapes, sizes, and composition—can all live under the general and uninformative map designation of "forest."

3. "Since jungle warfare so favours the attacker, a purely defensive battle in the jungle is doomed to disaster and must not be tolerated." *Military Training Pamphlet No. 2, Warfare in the Far East, Provisional* (London: War Office, 1944). This British view was, of course, based on vast countrywide areas of jungle.

2. WARFARE BEFORE FIREARMS

1. Recent research confirms the Osnabrück site. Earlier the battle was thought to have taken place near Detmold where, in the nineteenth century, a vast monument to commemorate the battle was erected.

The best description of the battle remains that of E. Creasy, *Fifteen Decisive Battles of the Western World* (London: Macmillan, 1906), chap. 5. Also useful is Bryan Perret's "The Massacre of the Legions," in Michael Stephenson, ed., *Battlegrounds: Geography and the History of Warfare* (Washington, DC: National Geographic, n.d.), pp. 94–98.

2. H. Mattingley, trans., *Tacitus on Britain and Germany: A New Translation* (West Drayton, UK: Penguin Books, 1948), pp. 84–88.

3. This term is not to be confused with the Finnish word *motti,* used in the 1939–40 Winter War and described in chapter 9 of this volume.

4. Charles Oman's *A History of the Art of War: The Middle Ages from the Fourth to the Fourteenth Century* (London: Methuen, 1898), despite its age, is succinct, useful, and accurate; see pp. 398–406.

5. The battle is well described in ibid., pp. 648–53.

6. Detailed accounts of the battle from different perspectives appear in Matthew Bennett, *Agincourt 1415: Triumph against the Odds* (London: Osprey, 1991); and John Keegan, "Agincourt," in *The Face of Battle* (London: Jonathan Cape, 1976), chap. 3.

7. The best modern account of Morat is a succinct and well-illustrated French-language monograph by Pierre Streit titled *Morat (1476), L'Indépendance des cantons suissses* (Paris: Economica, 2009). A useful brief English-language account is in David Chandler, ed., *A Traveller's Guide to the Battlefields of Europe*, vol. 2 (London: Hugh Evelyn, 1965), pp. 147–48.

8. Panigarola to the Duke of Milan, 25 June 1476, reproduced in full, in French, in Streit, *Morat,* chap. 12.

9. Chandler, *Traveller's Guide,* 1:135–36. Some of the Scotsmen may have possessed firearms.

3. EARLY MODERN WARFARE, 1500–1713

1. Accounts of the battle appear in Chandler, *Traveller's Guide,* 2:43–45; William P. Guthrie, *The Later Thirty Years War* (Westport, CT: Greenwood, 2003), pp. 54–59; C. V. Wedgewood, *The Thirty Years War* (London: Penguin, 1952), pp. 366–67; and Peter H. Wilson, *Europe's Tragedy: A History of the Thirty Years War* (London: Allen Lane, 2009), pp. 580–83.

2. Numerous accounts of the Battle of Malplaquet exist. Among the most useful are those that appear in David Chandler, *Marlborough as Military Commander* (London: Batsford, 1973), pp. 254–66; and J. R. Jones, *Marlborough* (Cambridge: Cambridge University Press, 1993), pp. 177–83.

3. Comte Turpin de Crissé, *Essai sur l'art de la guerre* (in French), 2 vols. (Paris: Prault and Joubert, 1754). Copies of the two volumes are held in the Library of the Royal Military Academy Sandhurst, Camberley, England. This book is written in elegant eighteenth-century French but includes some words and phrases no longer used in modern French.

For details on de Crissé's career and writings, see Philippe Richardot, "La Reception de Végère au XVIII siècle, Turpin de Crissé," in *Stratégique* 76, no. 4 (2010): 17–51. De Crissé made a special study of the Roman military writer Publius Flavius Renatus Vegetius, the author of *De Re Militairi.*

4. THE EIGHTEENTH CENTURY

1. Some of these units became absorbed into existing standing armies, losing their special roles, most notably in the British Army's Light Infantry and Rifle regiments which, though priding themselves on their bugles, green uniforms, and quick marching pace, became otherwise identical to other infantry regiments.

2. Accounts of these battles may be found in Christopher Duffy, *Frederick the Great, A Military Life* (London: Routledge, 1985), p. 174 (Hochkirch), pp. 210–18 (Torgau).

3. Ibid., p. 319.

4. A description quoted from an earlier work by A. G. Bradley, *Fight with France for North America,* quoted in John W. Burrows, *The Essex Regiment, 1st Battalion (44th)* (John W. Burrows, 1923), p. 9.

5. Francis Parkman, *Montcalm and Wolfe,* vol. 2 (Boston: Little, Brown, 1917), 147.

6. The battle is well described in Ruth Sheppard, ed., *Empires Collide: The French and India War, 1754–63* (Oxford: Osprey, 2007), pt. 1. Thomas E. Crocker, in *Braddock's March* (New York: Westholme, 2009), argues that the battle was truly decisive in that if Braddock had won, the Seven Years' War that followed would not have lasted so long in North America and the taxes needed to pay for it, a major cause of the third war, the American War of Independence, would not have been imposed.

7. William Smith, *Historical Account of Bouquet's Expedition against the Ohio Indians in 1764*, Ohio Valley Historical Series 1 (Cincinnati: Robert Clarke, 1868), pp. 107–108. This work was originally published in Philadelphia in 1765, was republished in Cincinnati by Robert Clarke in 1868, and was published again by University Microfilm International, Ann Arbor, Michigan, in 1881.

8. The Royal American Regiment became, briefly, the 62nd Foot, the 60th Foot, and later the King's Royal Rifle Corps.

9. For details of the early history of the Royal American Regiment, see Lewis Butler, *The Annals of the King's Royal Rifle Corps* (London: Smith Elder, 1913), introduction, chap. 1.

10. This corps was issued with muskets cut down to make carbines. The number eighty was used again later for two regiments raised in Britain. The second of these became a battalion of the South Staffordshire Regiment. The existence of this American unit is recorded in Colonel W. L. Vale, *The History of the South Staffordshire Regiment* (Aldershot: Gale and Polden, 1923), p.33, and is only noted here to avoid confusion.

11. Butler, *Annals*, pp. 160–61.

12. For excerpts from Bouquet's instructions, see ibid., appendix 4, pp. 330–34. Bouquet, commanding a battalion in a 1758 advance on Fort Duquesne, sent sixteen men with rifle-barreled "fuzils" into woods in pairs for flank screening.

13. Ibid., pp. 162–66, 187–89.

14. "It is everywhere hilly and covered with wood interspersed by ravines, creeks and marshy ground and every quarter of a mile is a post fit for ambuscades . . . every hundred yards might be dispatch." General Grey, quoted in Michael Foss, *The Royal Fusiliers* (London: Hamish Hamilton, 1967), p. 44.

15. For a useful account, see Franklin B. Wickwire and Mary B. Wickwire, *Cornwallis and the War of Independence* (London: Faber and Faber, 1970), pp. 205–16.

16. François Furet and Denis Richet, *The French Revolution*, trans. Stephen Hardman (New York: Macmillan, 1970), pp. 240–41, 274–75, 281, 365, 367, 382–83.

17. F. Gunther Eyck, *Loyal Rebels: Andreas Hofer and the Tyrolean Uprising of 1809* (Lanham, MD: University Press of America, 1986), p. 168. Hofer, betrayed, captured and executed, remains an iconic figure in Tyrolean history.

18. The battle is described in Marcus Cunliffe, *The Royal Irish Fusiliers, 1793–1950* (Oxford: Oxford University Press, 1952), pp. 95–102; and Andrew Rawson, *The Peninsula War: A Battlefield Guide* (Barnsley, UK: Pen and Sword, 2009), pp. 131–40.

19. Andrew Zamoyski, *1812: Napoleon's Fatal March on Moscow* (London: Harper Collins, 2004), p. 93.

20. Ibid., pp. 381–82.

21. For a useful summary of this writing on British and European light troops, see David Gates, *The British Light Infantry Arm, 1790–1815: Its Creation, Training and Operational Role* (London: Batsford, 1987).

22. Carl von Clausewitz, *On War*, trans. Michael Howard and Peter Paret (Princeton, NJ: Princeton University Press, 1976), pp. 452, 543–44.

5. TOWARD LATER MODERN WARFARE, 1815–1914

1. The problem of cohesion may have been reduced for some New York regiments that, in emulation of the famous French Algerian regiment, wore the distinctive, and easily recognizable, scarlet baggy trousers of the Zouaves.

2. Libraries of books have been written on the fighting in the American Civil War. For a reliable account with details of commanders, formations, and units, see William C. Davis, *The Battlefields of the Civil War* (London: Salamander, 1989); chaps. 7 and 11 cover Charlottesville and the Wilderness, respectively.

3. For a detailed and definitive account of this battle, see Robert Garth Scott, *Into the Wilderness with the Army of the Potomac* (Bloomington: Indiana University Press, 1985). This work also contains remarkable photographs taken during or just after the battle.

4. Ibid., p. 182.

5. A detailed account of the battle is in Gordon A. Craig, *The Battle of Königgratz* (London: Weidenfeld and Nicolson, 1965). The battle was fought between the village of Sadowa and the small town then known as Königgratz, now Hradec Kralove.

6. Craig, *Königgratz*, pp. 113–14.

7. The colonel, Suzzoni, was killed and the Tirrailleurs unit, after fighting tenaciously, was wiped out. One sergeant, Abd el Kader ben Dekish, gained a lasting place in French military history by saving the regiment's banner. General R. Huré, ed., *L'Armeé d'Afrique, 1840–1962* (Paris: Lavauzelle, 1972), pp. 133–34.

8. William Serman and Jean Paul Bertaud, *Nouvelle histoire militaire de la France, 1789–1919* (Paris: Fayard, 1998), p. 437.

9. Michael Howard, *The Franco-Prussian War* (London: Methuen, 1981), pp. 249–56, 289, 296, 377. The activities of the *francs-tireurs* came to lead to German reprisals, communal punishment fines, or the burning of houses and villages.

10. Lieutenant-Colonel H. Schaw, *Defence and Attack of Positions and Localities* (London: Mitchell, 1875), chap. 9.

11. Schaw included an appendix-type note on tree felling, interesting for the light it throws on the technology of the 1870s. The note asserted that two skilled men could fell up to 150 fir trees, with trunks one foot in diameter, per day, or one every five minutes. An oak or other hard-wood tree might take fifteen minutes, or between 30 and 40 per day. The trimming of branches could take as long as felling trees, although cross-cutting trees into lengths took only half this time. Unskilled labor would only accomplish between one-third and one-half a day's work. Larger trees would take more time and required more men for the work.

12. Colonel Robert Home, *A Précis of Modern Tactics,* revised by Lieutenant-Colonel Sisson C. Pratt (London: Her Majesty's Stationery Office, 1892), p. xi.

6. THE FIRST WORLD WAR, 1914–17

1. Alexander Solzhenitsyn, *August 1914,* trans. Michael Glenny (London: Book Club Associates, 1971), pp. 463–64.

2. The event is described in Lyn Macdonald, *1914* (London: Michael Joseph, 1987), pp. 265–67.

3. Brigadier-General A. W. Hussey and Major D. S. Inman, *The Fifth Division in the Great War* (London: Nisbet, 1921), p. 24.

4. The event is recorded in Captain Cyril Falls, *Life of a Regiment*, Vol. 4, *The Gordon Highlanders in the First World War, 1914–1919* (Aberdeen, Scotland: Aberdeen University Press, 1958), pp. 19–20. The wood had temporarily acquired an English name, "Shrewsbury Wood." Rapid rifle fire by well-trained regular soldiers of the time could be as much as fifteen rounds a minute.

5. Geoffrey Evans, *Tannenberg* (London: Hamish Hamilton, 1970), pp. 153–54. Evans follows an account of this tragedy given by Samsonov's chief of staff General Postovski. Solzhenitsyn, in *August 1914*, pp. 148–49, writes a moving literary account.

6. In the British Army the lighter Lewis gun remained standard at battalion level, but the earlier versions required trolleys for ammunition supply. The heavier Vickers machine gun was redistributed to companies of a Machine Gun Corps attached to brigades. There were three types of mortar: the light 3-inch Stokes at brigade level, the not very satisfactory larger medium 6-inch at division level, and the 9.45-inch at corps level. Mortars were not constituted into a special corps or regiment. The effect of these weapons, together with that of the French 37-mm. trench gun and the flame-thrower, was to make the platoon rather than the company the base for infantry tactics.

7. Hughes, *Mametz*, provides a detailed and critical account of this battle from a soldier's point of view. An officer's account appears in Llewelyn Wyn Griffith, *Up to Mametz and Beyond* (Barnsley, UK: Pen and Sword, 2010). The Welsh poet David Jones, in his *In Parenthesis*, wrote of his own experience at Mametz: "And to your front stretched long laterally, and receded deeply, the dark wood."

8. This event is recorded in A. H. Farrar-Hockley, *The Somme* (London: Batsford, 1964), pp. 162–63.

9. G. D. Sheffield, *The Somme* (London: Cassell, 2003), p. 121, notes a barrage of 750 mortar bombs in fifteen minutes.

10. E. G. Vanlint, *Tommy Jim in Flanders Fields* (London: Army Benevolent Fund, 2007), p. 164.

11. Captain B. H. Liddell Hart, *The Tanks*, vol. 1 (London: Cassell, 1959), p. 75. One may speculate that tree stumps provided the design for later antitank obstacles.

12. A remarkable photograph of South African infantrymen entering this last battered section of the wood appears in Ian Uys, *Delville Wood* (Johannesburg: Uys Publishers, 1983), pp. 32–33.

13. Lieutenant-Colonel Graham Seton Hutchinson, *The Thirty-Third Division in France and Flanders, 1915–1919* (privately published, n.d.), p. 16, records one brigade commander asking for an artillery bombardment of the wood and receiving the reply, "Nothing can live there, my dear fellow, nothing lives there." The author then added, "We were to prove the truth of these words."

14. Ibid., p. 17.

15. Chandler, *Battlefields of Europe*, 1:109.

16. The pictures appear in *Verdun-Argonne, 1914–18*, a Michelin guidebook (Clermont-Ferrand, UK: Michelin, 1931); see, respectively, pp. 15, 16, 25, 41, 45, 122, 145, and 150.

17. Arnold Zweig, "De vieilles raciness aux doigt gris s'enchevêtrent . . . Abattus vers le sol . . . Ici, l'homme en quelques mois a ravagé ce que la nature avait élaboré pendant des générations d'hommes," quoted in "1916–2006, Ceux de Verdun, Les chemins de la mémoire", *Le Figaro* (2006): 18–19.

18. The battle is described in greater detail in Jack Horsfall and Nigel Cave, *Bourlon Wood* (Barnsley, UK: Leo Cooper, 2002). The work includes a photograph of two tanks knocked out in the wood (pp. 106–107).

19. Hussey and Inman, in *The Fifth Division*, pp. 210–11, note the need to evacuate an infected area by sprinkling any cavity or crater with chloride of lime and then covering it over with earth. The Royal Army Medical Corps mounted "gas patrols" to warn troops of the dangers and to fill in the holes.

7. THE FIRST WORLD WAR, 1918

1. For an excellent account of the Battle of Belleau Wood, see Oliver L. Spalding and John W. Wright, *The Second Division, American Expeditionary Force in France, 1917–1919* (New York: Hillman, 1937), pp. 48–70. A shorter but useful account appears in David Bonk, *Chateau-Thierry and Belleau Wood, 1918* (Oxford: Osprey, 2007). The French had to supply the American divisions with some three thousand guns and two thousand aircraft.

2. German casualties are reckoned for the wider sector. Martin Gilbert notes that in a nearby cemetery there are 8,624 graves. See Gilbert, *The First World War* (London: Weidenfeld, 1988), p. 435.

3. Before Belleau Wood, the U.S. Marines had been regarded poorly by the U.S. Army, as men suitable only for landings from warships in a warm climate. Belleau Wood was to make the Army-Marine rivalry one on equal terms.

4. These events are described in a privately published work by General Mangin's son; see Louis-Eugène Mangin, *Le Général Mangin* (1990), pp. 325–30. The divided views of the two French commanders are noteworthy. Foch specifically ordered Mangin to maintain the momentum of the attack. The effect on the morale of the French soldiers was considerable.

5. General Braithwaite, commander of the 62nd Division, observed, "I have seen nothing thicker since I fought thirty-five years ago in the Burma jungle." See Everard Wyrall, *The History of the 62nd (West Riding) Division, 1914–18* (London: John Lane and Bodley Head, n.d.), p. 178.

6. The battle is described in Brigadier-General Sir James E. Edmonds, *Military Operations, France and Belgium 1918* (London: Macmillan, 1939), chaps. 13–17; Falls, *Gordon Highlander,* chap. 19; Wyrall, *62nd Division,* chaps. 16–18, with some additional detail in Captain E. V. Tempest, *History of the Sixth Battalion West Yorkshire Regiment* (Leeds: Henry Walker and Bradford D. Wilson, 1941), pp. 52–54.

7. These excerpts from the diary of an officer of the Eighth Battalion of the West Yorkshire Regiment are quoted in Wyrall, *West Riding Division*, pp. 180–81. They provide a lively firsthand account of the confusion into which forest warfare can fall.

8. *Report of the Committee on the Lessons of the Great War* (London: War Office, 1932). The committee was composed of a lieutenant-general as chairman, five major-generals, and two brigadiers.

8. THE SECOND WORLD WAR, 1939–45

1. The term "Molotov Cocktail," used to describe homemade grenades made from inflammable fluids with a simple hand fuse all in a jar or bottle, first appeared in this conflict. Molotov Cocktails could cause temporary blindness or start a fire inside a tank.

2. An account of these battles appears in Anthony E. Upton, *Finland, 1939–1940* (London: Davis-Poynter, 1974), pp. 86–89. Also useful, especially for details, is Philip Jowett and Brent Snodgrass, *Finland at War, 1939–45* (Oxford: Osprey, 2006), pp. 6–11, 42–45.

3. These campaigns are analyzed in two of the most informative history texts on the practicalities of forest warfare: *Terrain Factors in the Russian Campaign* compiled by the Center of Military History, Washington, DC, in 1986; and Jesse W. Miller, "Forest Fighting on the Eastern Front in World War II," *Geographical Review* 62 (1972): 186–208.

4. A noteworthy photograph, picturing a convict dressed in black to show up against the snow, standing in the front of a forest to draw enemy machine-gun fire and thus reveal the enemy's location, appears in *50 let sovietskikh vooruzhennikh sil, photodokumenty* [Fifty Years of Soviet Armed Forces, Photodocuments] (Moscow: Military Publishing House, 1967).

5. John Erickson, *The Road to Berlin*, 2 vols. (London: Weidenfeld and Nicolson, 1983), and David M. Glantz and Jonathan House, *When Titans Clashed* (Lawrence: University Press of Kansas, 1995), remain the finest accounts of all the military operations. Alan Clark, *Barbarossa: The Russian-German Conflict, 1941–45* (New York: Morrow, 1985 [1965]), provides a useful general popular account especially with reference to partisans; for a clear discussion of the political dimension of the partisans' activity, see the Penguin edition, pp. 183–86. Also valuable, incorporating some later revisions, is Duncan Anderson, Lloyd Clark, and Stephen Walsh, *The Eastern Front (Campaigns of World War II)* (Newton Abbot, UK: David and Charles, 2001).

6. As quoted in Anderson, Clark, and Walsh, *Eastern Front*, p. 38, "tempers began to fray with unnerving rapidity."

7. A general account of *maquis* activities appears in Matthew Cobb, *The Resistance: The French Fight against the Nazis* (London: Simon and Schuster, 2009), chap. 7.

8. Cobb, *Resistance*, pp. 105–106, notes the need for moonlight and clear weather. The aircraft generally used was a slow single-engine monoplane, the Westland Lysander designed in the 1930s for cooperation with the army and capable of landing and taking off in small spaces with uneven ground.

9. Martin Middlebrook, *Arnham 1944: : The Airborne Battle, 17–26 September* (London: Penguin Books, 1995), pp. 139–40, both quotations. Middlebrook's book is an excellent account of the whole battle and the valor of the British and Polish soldiers. The account here must necessarily be limited to the fighting in the woods.

10. Useful accounts of the Ardennes battles in the wider context appear in James Arnold, *Ardennes 1944* (London: Osprey, 1980); H. Cole, *The Ardennes: Battle of the Bulge* (Washington, DC: Department of the Army, 1965); and J. Pimlott, *Battle of the Bulge* (New York, Bison, 1984).

11. The major work on the battle is Edward G. Miller, *A Dark Bloody Ground: The Hürtgen Forest and the Roer River Dams, 1944–1945* (College Station: Texas A&M University Press, 1995). Also useful are Charles Whiting, *The Battle of Hürtgen Forest* (Staplehurst, UK: Spellmount, 2000); and Robert Stirling Rush, *Hell in Hürtgen Forest* (Lawrence: University Press of Kansas, 2001). Adolf Hohenstein and Wolfgang Trees, *Hölle im Hürtgenwald*, (Aachen, Germany: Triangle, 1981), is a well-illustrated and documented German-language account.

12. An American soldier remarked that all they "ever saw was wild deer and jerries, and trees, firebreaks and more trees" (Miller, *Dark Bloody Ground*, p. 44). Soldiers complained of the gloomy "sameness."

13. Ibid., p. 108. British readers of American accounts may experience some surprise as these accounts refer to soldiers covering the mines with their "mess kit"—in British Army parlance, their evening dress uniform, not to be confused with "mess tins."

14. Ibid., p. 29.

15. The larger formations included, at different times, the 12th, 47th, 273rd, and 277th *Volgrenadier* Divisions, the 85th, 89th, 275th, 344th, and 353rd Infantry Divisions, the 3rd Parachute Division, and the 116th Panzer Division. Only a few of them, even at the outset, were anywhere near full strength or complete equipment.

16. Among some soldiers, there also appeared to be a reluctance to make any close friendships with new replacements, as they believed that these new arrivals, lacking experience, would be the first to be killed.

17. Several letters in a posthumous collection of Maréchal de Lattre's correspondence in these months provide some detail of their operations. See Maréchal Jean de Lattre, *Reconquérir, Écrits, 1944–45* (Paris: Plon, 1985). Huré's *Armée d'Afrique*, pp. 404–18, concentrates on the North African units.

9. POST-1945 AND CONCLUSION

1. For example, Richard Simpkin, a British Army brigadier, wrote of the helicopter that it "allows you to use ground tactically without depending on it for mobility." Simpkin, *The Race to the Swift* (London: Brassey's, 1985), p. 76.

An American herbicide, Agent Orange, was developed for deforestation in the 1960s, for use when a wooded area presented a serious impediment. Napalm, used elsewhere, was of only limited effect when dropped on green foliage.

2. Much useful information on the Chechnya operations may be found in Lieutenant-Colonel C. W. Blandy, *North Caucasus: Problems of Helicopter Support in Mountains* (Swindon, UK: Defence Academy of the United Kingdom, 2007).

3. Michael Orr, "Better or Just Not So Bad, an Evaluation of Russian Combat Efficiency in the Second Chechen War," and Lester W. Grau "Technology and the Second Chechen Campaign," both in Anne Aldis, ed., *The Second Chechen War* (Swindon, UK: Strategic and Combat Studies Institute, 2000), pp. 84–112.

4. This observation is recorded in Michael Jones, *The Retreat: Hitler's First Defeat* (London: John Murray, 2009), pp. 108–109.

5. Teilhard de Chardin, "Seul la figure de Christ peut recueillir, exprimer et consoler ce qu'il y a d'horreur, d'espérance et de profonde mystère dane un pareil dechaînement de lutte et d'horreur," quoted in Huré, *Armée d'Afrique*, p. 291.

6. Siegfried Sassoon, *Memoirs of an Infantry Officer* (London: Faber and Faber, 1930), p. 64.

7. See chapter 6, note 17.

SELECT BIBLIOGRAPHY

PUBLISHED BOOKS

Aldis, Anne, ed. *The Second Chechen War.* Swindon, UK: Strategic and Combat Studies Institute, 2000.

Anderson, Duncan, Lloyd Clark, and Stephen Walsh. *The Eastern Front (Campaigns of World War II).* Newton Abbot, UK: David and Charles, 2001.

Arnold, James. *Ardennes 1944.* London: Osprey, 1980.

Bennett, Matthew. *Agincourt 1415, Triumph against the Odds.* London: Osprey, 1991.

Blandy, Lieutenant-Colonel C.W. *North Caucasus, Problems of Helicopter Support in Mountains.* Swindon, UK: Defence Academy of the United Kingdom, 2007.

Bonk, David. *Chateau-Thierry and Belleau Wood, 1918.* Oxford: Osprey, 2007.

Butler, L. *The Annals of the King's Royal Rifle Corps.* London: Smith Elder, 1913.

Chandler, David. *A Traveller's Guide to the Battlefields of Europe.* 2 vols. London: Hugh Evelyn, 1965.

Chandler, David. *.Marlborough as Military Commander.* London: Batsford, 1973.

Clark, Alan. *Barbarossa: The Russian German Conflict, 1941–45.* New York: Morrow, 1985 [1965].

Clausewitz, Carl von. *On War.* Trans. Michael Howard and Peter Paret. Princeton, NJ: Princeton University Press, 1976.

Cobb, Matthew. *The Resistance: The French Fight against the Nazis.* London: Simon and Schuster, 2004.

Cole, H. *The Ardennes: Battle of the Bulge.* Washington, DC: Department of the Army, 1965.

Craig, Gordon A. *The Battle of Königgratz.* London: Weidenfeld, 1965.

Creasy, E. *Fifteen Decisive Battles of the Modern World.* London: Macmillan, 1906.

Crocker, Thomas E. *Braddock's March.* New York: Westholme, 2009.

Cunliffe, Marcus. *The Royal Irish Fusiliers, 1795–1950.* Oxford: Oxford University Press, 1952.

Davis, William C. *The Battlefields of the Civil War.* London: Salamander, 1989.

De Crissé, Comte Turpin, *Essai sur l'art de guerre.* In French. Paris: Prault and Joubert, 1754.

De Lattre, Maréchal Jean *Reconquérir, Écrits, 1944–45.* Paris: Plon, 1985.

Duffy, Christopher. *Frederick the Great: A Military Life.* London: Routledge, 1985.

Edmonds, Brigadier-General Sir James E. *Military Operations, France and Belgium 1918.* London: Macmillan, 1939.

Erickson, John. *The Road to Berlin.* London: Weidenfeld and Nicolson, 1983.

Evans, Geoffrey. *Tannenberg.* London: Hamish Hamilton, 1976.

Eyck, F. Gunther. *Loyal Rebels: Andreas Hofer and the Tyrolean Uprising of 1809*. Lanham, MD: University Press of America, 1986.

Falls, Captain Cyril. *Life of a Regiment*. Vol. 4, *The History of the Gordon Highlanders in the First World War, 1914–1919*. Aberdeen, Scotland: Aberdeen University Press, 1958.

Farvar-Hockley, A. H. *The Somme*. London: Batsford, 1969.

Foss, Michael *The Royal Fusiliers*. London: Hamish Hamilton, 1967.

Furet, François, and Denis Richet. *The French Revolution*. Trans. Stephen Hardigan. New York: Macmillan, 1970.

Gates, David. *The British Light Infantry Arm, 1790–1815: Its Creation, Training and Operational Role*. London: Batsford, 1987.

Gilbert, Martin. *The First World War*. London: Weidenfeld, 1988.

Glantz, David M., and Jonathan House. *When Titans Clash*. Lawrence: University Press of Kansas, 1995.

Guthrie, William B. *The Later Thirty Years War*. Westport, CT: Greenwood, 2003.

Hohenstein, Adolf, and Wolfgang Trees. *Hölle im Hürtgenwald*. In German. Aachen, Germany: Triangle, 1981.

Home, Colonel Robert. *A Précis of Modern Tactics*. Revised by Lieutenant-Colonel Sisson C. Pratt. London: Her Majesty's Stationery Office, 1892.

Horsfall, Jack, and Nigel Cave. *Bourlon Wood*. Barnsley, UK: Leo Cooper, 2002.

Howard, Michael. *The Franco-Prussian War*. London: Methuen, 1981.

Hughes, Colin, *Mametz: Lloyd George's Welsh Army at the Battle of the Somme,* Norwich, UK: Gliddon Books, 1990.

Huré, General R., ed. *L'Armée d'Afrique, 1830–1962*. Paris: Lavauzelle, 1977.

Hussey, Brigadier-General A. W., and Major D. S. Inman. *The Fifth Division in the Great War*. London: Nisbet, 1921.

Jones, Michael. *The Retreat: Hitler's First Defeat*. London: John Murray, 2004.

Jones, J. R. *Marlborough*. Cambridge: Cambridge University Press, 1993.

Jowett, Philip, and Brent Snodgrass. *Finland at War, 1939–45*. Oxford: Osprey, 2006.

Keegan, John. *The Face of Battle*. London: Jonathan Cape, 1976.

Liddell Hart, Captain B. H. *The Tanks*. Vol. 1. London: Cassell, 1959.

Macdonald, Lyn. *1914*. London: Michael Joseph, 1987.

Mangin, Louis-Eugène. *Le Général Mangin*. Privately published, 1980.

Mattingley, H., trans. *Tacitus on Britain and Germany: A New Translation*. West Drayton, UK: Penguin Books, 1948.

Middlebrook, Martin. *Arnhem 1944: The Airborne Battle, 17–26 September*. London: Penguin Books, 1995.

Miller, Edward G. *A Dark Bloody Ground: The Hürtgen Forest and the Roer River Dams, 1944–1945*. College Station: Texas A&M University Press, 1995.

Oman, Charles. *A History of the Art of War: The Middle Ages from the Fourth to the Fourteenth Century*. London: Methuen, 1898.

Pimlott, John. *Battle of the Bulge*. New York: Bison, 1984.

Rawson, Andrew. *The Peninsula War: A Battlefield Guide*. Barnsley, UK: Pen and Sword, 2009.

Rush, Robert Stirling. *Hell in Hürtgen Forest*. Lawrence: University Press of Kansas, 2001.

Sassoon, Siegfried. *Memoirs of an Infantry Officer*. London: Faber and Faber, 1930.

Schaw, Lieutenant-Colonel H. *Defence and Attack of Positions and Localities*. London: Mitchell, 1875.

Scott, Robert Garth. *Into the Wilderness with the Army of the Potomac.* Bloomington: Indiana University Press, 1985.

Serman, William, and Jean Paul Bertaud. *Nouvelle histoire militaire de la France, 1789–1919.* Paris: Fayard, 1998.

Hutchinson, Lieutenant-Colonel Graham Seton. *The Thirty-Third Division in France and Flanders, 1915–1919.* Privately published, n.d.

Spalding, Oliver L., and John W. Wright. *The Second Division: American Expeditionary Force in France, 1917–1919.* New York: Hillman, 1937.

Stephenson, Michael, ed. *Battlegrounds: Geography and the History of Warfare.* Washington, DC: National Geographic Society, n.d.

Streit, Pierre. *Morat (1476) L'Indépendance des cantons suisses.* Paris : Economica, 2006.

Tempest, Captain E. V. *History of the Sixth Battalion West Yorkshire Regiment.* Leeds, UK: Henry Walker and Bradford D. Wilson, 1941.

Upton, Anthony E. *Finland, 1939–40.* London: Davis-Poynter, 1974.

Valint, E. G. *Tommy Jim in Flanders Fields.* London: Army Benevolent Fund, 2007.

Verdun, Argonne 1914–18. Michelin Guidebook. Clermont Ferrand, UK: Michelin, 1931.

Wedgewood, C. V. *The Thirty Years War.* London: Penguin, 1952.

Whiting, Charles. *The Battle of Hürtgen Forest.* Staplehurst, UK: Spellmount, 2000.

Wickwire, Franklin B., and Mary B. Wickwire. *Cornwallis and the War of Independence.* London: Faber and Faber, 1970.

Wilson, Peter H. *Europe's Tragedy: A History of the Thirty Years War.* London: Allen Lane, 2009

Wyn Griffith, Llewelyn. *Up to Mametz and Beyond.* Barnsley, South Yorkshire: Pen and Sword, 2010.

Wyrall, Everard. *The History of the 62nd (West Riding) Division, 1914–18.* London: John Lane and Bodley Head, n.d.

ARTICLES AND PAPERS

Centre of Military History. *Terrain Factors in the Russia Campaign.* Washington, DC, 1986.

50 let sovietskikh vooruzhennikh sil, photodokumenty [Fifty Years of Soviet Armed Forces, Photodocuments]. Moscow: Military Publishing House, 1967.

Military Training Pamphlet. No. 2, *Warfare in the Far East, Provisional.* London: War Office, 1944.

Miller, Jesse W. "Forest Fighting on the Eastern Front in World War II." *Geographical Review* 62 (1972): 186–208.

"1916–2006 Ceux de Verdun, Les Chemins de la memoire," *Le Figaro* (2000): 18–19.

Report on the Lessons of the Great War. London: War Office, 1932.

INDEX

ANTHONY CLAYTON,

now retired, was an official of the British Colonial Government of Kenya until independence; served in the British Army's reserve Territorial Army in the infantry and Intelligence Corps; was Senior Lecturer at the Royal Military Academy Sandhurst; was librarian of the Conflict Studies Research Center; and Associate Lecturer at the University of Surrey. He is author of fifteen books, most recently *Paths of Glory: The French Army, 1914–1918*; *The British Officer: Leaders of the Army from 1660 to the Present*; *Defeat: When Nations Lose a War*; and a chapter on the wars of decolonization in volume 4 of the forthcoming *Cambridge History of War*.